INSIDE THE VAULT

The True Story of a Master Bank Burglar

Amil Dinsio

Copyright © 2013 I Love You Brother, LLC

All rights reserved. No part of this book may be used or reproduced in any manner whatsoever without prior written consent of the publisher except in the case of brief quotations embodied in critical articles and reviews. Special book excerpts or customized printings can be created to fit specific needs.

Published by:
I Love You Brother, LLC

For information contact:
amildinsio@gmail.com

ISBN hardcover:978-1-939758-04-0
ISBN eBook: 978-1-939758-05-7

For James,
I love you brother.

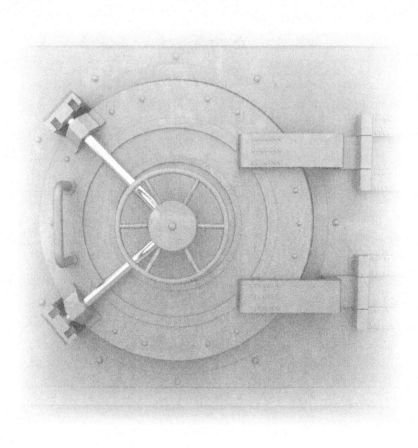

Contents

vii	*Introduction*
1	Chapter 1: **How It All Began**
9	Chapter 2: **The Score**
17	Chapter 3: **Westward Bound**
33	Chapter 4: **Prep Time**
41	Chapter 5: **Good to Go**
51	Chapter 6: **Where No Thief Has Gone Before**
65	Chapter 7: **A Weekend in the Vault**
81	Chapter 8: **The Loot in Las Vegas**
91	Chapter 9: **Robber's Roost**
97	Chapter 10: **Lordstown**
113	Chapter 11: **The Heat Is On**
121	Chapter 12: **The Frame-up**
133	Chapter 13: **The Lordstown Trial**
149	*Epilogue: Once a Thief, Always a Thief*
159	*Photographs*

*When this is all over,
I'll give you a story.
I'll give you a real story.*

Amil Dinsio speaking to the media, 1972

Introduction

Forty years later, I'm giving you the real story. I'm giving you the story of the greatest bank burglary in American history. I'm giving you this story because it is MY story to give.

Books have been written and television documentaries have been made about the burglary of President Richard Nixon's money that netted over twelve million dollars, but none of those accounts are accurate.

They are inaccurate because no one knows the real story, the whole story; no one, that is, except for me.

And now you will know what people have speculated about—and never figured out—for forty years. You will know how I planned the burglary of the United California Bank in Laguna Niguel, California. You will know exactly how my crew and I blasted through the roof of the vault and how we looted the contents of hundreds of safe deposit boxes over the weekend of March 24, 1972.

The FBI refers to me as a master bank burglar—the best in the world, even. I don't see myself that way, though. I see myself as just an average guy. I see myself as a husband, father, grandfather, son, brother, and friend.

But, in all fairness to the FBI, I have pulled off over a hundred successful bank burglaries, so I guess I am a master at my chosen craft.

I am a criminal. I'm not necessarily proud of that fact, but I am what I am and there's no denying it.

However, my crew and I weren't the only crooks involved in this burglary and its aftermath. You see, the government wasn't smart enough to catch me honestly. They had to lie, steal, and plant evidence to convict me.

The federal agents, prosecutors, and judges are criminals far bigger than I, because they were sworn to uphold the law and defend the Constitution of the United States. I admit what I am, but they have never admitted to being criminals.

I have changed some names in this book to protect the innocent. However, I have identified all federal agents, prosecutors, and judges accurately.

After all, the criminals should have to face the music—all of us, including the criminals who carry badges and wear black robes.

CHAPTER ONE

How It All Began

"Nobody move and nobody gets hurt!"

I can still remember yelling those words as my brother James and I ran, guns drawn, through the back door of that very first bank so many years ago in Wheeling, West Virginia. My brother gathered together seven of the eight people in the bank, and I told the eighth one, a teller, to give me all the money in the drawers. She easily complied, and less than two minutes later, we ran back out the same back door more than twenty-two thousand dollars richer.

I was only sixteen years old.

I was born in Goshen, Ohio, in 1936, and I was the seventh of my parents' eight children. My father immigrated to America from Italy when he was just seventeen years old, coming through Ellis Island in New York with only twelve dollars in his pocket. When my father came to America, he was accompanied by a Sicilian friend named Jimmy Prato. Jimmy later became a mob boss, and went by the name of "Two Gun Jimmy." I knew him very well, and was close to his nephew, Lenny Strollo. Lenny was just an underboss, doing whatever Two Gun Jimmy told him to do. My father always told my brother and me to stay away from Two Gun Jimmy, and never to do anything illegal for him or the mob. My father told us that the mob just uses people to do their dirty work.

Growing up, we were poor—as poor as poor can get. We lived on a small 90-acre farm in Goshen Township, Ohio. Our home was tiny. The kitchen was only about twenty-five by twenty-five feet, with a big table in the middle. The house had two bedrooms. One was about the size of the kitchen, and at one time or another, all eight of us kids slept in that one bedroom. My mother and father slept in the other small bedroom. The house had no running water or electricity. Our water came from a hand pump that pumped water up from a well to the sink in the kitchen. My mother cooked on a coal stove, and that same coal stove heated our home in the wintertime. Our house was lit using kerosene lamps. In one small room, we had a big radio hooked up to a car battery.

Although we were very poor, one thing we always had was food. We had a good-sized barn on the farm with milking cows, pigs, goats, chickens, ducks, etc. My father did the butchering, and the meat was stored in a freezer house rental room in Salem, Ohio. He would smoke the pork, bacon, and hams in a smokehouse down by the barn. We had a big garden, and my mother canned bottle after bottle of garden crops, with help from us kids. We had a large peach orchard as well, and my mother canned peaches too. In the basement under the house, we stored bins of apples, along with cider barrels and my father's elderberry wine.

The farm could not support the family, so both my parents had to work. While we lived on the farm, my father worked as a machinist at Morgan's Engineering in Alliance, Ohio, about fifteen miles from the farm. During World War II, my mother worked at the Mullin's Manufacturing in Salem, Ohio, making bathtubs and sinks.

I did well enough in school to get the grades necessary to play football and basketball. I was pretty good, too. To this day, my daughters kid me about the cheerleaders yelling "hubba-hubba, bing, bing, baby, you got everything," as I ran up and down the basketball court. Even now, I can still put a ball through a hoop better than most of my peers.

Up until the sixth grade, I went to a one-room school called Meadowbrook.

Then, in 1946, my dad sold the farm, and we moved to North Lima, Ohio—about six miles from Youngstown. There, my father built a small restaurant. My mother was the cook, and she was great at making tasty food.

In a back room of the restaurant, Two Gun Jimmy put in one-armed bandits—a.k.a. slot machines. Along with the one-armed bandits, my father set up poker tables in that back room. You see, back in the late 1940s and early '50s, the mob had the county sheriff, Sheriff Elser, on their side. My father was really good friends with Sheriff Elser, and the sheriff let the gambling go on. Almost every night, in that back room, big poker games were played. It was right up my alley. The guys called me Shorty and always had me running and getting them food and sodas while they played. They'd give me nickels and dimes in return, which I would then take right over to the one-armed bandits, pulling down the handle and losing my money. I was just a foolish kid. I loved it.

The restaurant had good business from the truckers who hauled cement and coal out of Bessemer, Pennsylvania. The road took them right past the restaurant, and they'd stop and eat my mother's delicious cooking. Then, the Ohio Water Service built a lake, and it shut off the road coming from Pennsylvania. That killed our business, and my family had to close the restaurant.

Whether at the restaurant, on the farm, or in school, my brothers and I were always the cool guys. If there was any ass-kicking to be done, the older Dinsio brothers could handle it, and as I got older, I could too. There was always an older Dinsio brother to take care of the younger, and the guys knew that.

My family was close, and we were always proud of each other's accomplishments. During the Second World War, two of my brothers, Vince and William, joined the Navy. I remember my mother hanging two small American flags in the window of the house to show that our home had men serving their country.

I love all my siblings, and the FBI has said that "the Dinsios are a fiercely loyal clan," but I was always closest to my brother James, who was seven years older than I. James was a good man, and always took care of my sisters and me. James and I weren't just brothers; our relationship was more unique than that. James was the closest person to me throughout my life. We thought alike; we worked well with each other; and we always defended and protected each other. Everyone knew that if they incurred the wrath of one of us, they incurred the wrath of both of us. It also was widely known that a situation like that never ended well for our enemy. Most importantly, James and I knew without a doubt, without a second's hesitation, each of us would take—or shoot—a bullet to protect the other one.

In 1951, James bought a 1950 Packard that he liked to drive to Steubenville, Ohio, and he often took me with him. When we would go to Steubenville, we would also stop to see the mob boss's son, Rab, whom my brother knew. Rab ran the Venetian Gardens, which was where the real mob guys hung out. On a couple of occasions, I even saw Dean Martin there—after all, he was good friends with Rab, and Steubenville was Dean's hometown.

Sometimes, we would go with Rab and a couple of his friends over the bridge into Wheeling, West Virginia. From there, we would head out into the country, to an old barn where they held rooster fights. Sometimes my brother would bet on a rooster to win. When the rooster lost, it was taken to a block of wood, where it would get its head cut off, blood flying everywhere. I really didn't like to see that happen, and neither did my brother; but he still liked to bet on the roosters.

After we left the rooster fights, we would stop in Wheeling, at a small hole-in-the-wall that sold real good hot sausage sandwiches and pizza. We would park the car right on the street, or alongside a small bank building. After a few nights looking at that bank, we started wondering whether we might be able to rob it. We figured, with all the steel workers in Wheeling cashing checks, we'd get a lot of money.

We walked around to the back of the bank to check it out. Behind the bank was a lot where the bank employees parked their cars. James checked the back door, and no lie—you could take a pen knife and slide the locking bolt back into the door frame and open the door. So one night, we went into the bank. We looked around, and then came back out. After that, we spent several nights lying out behind the back of the bank. As far as I can remember, not once did we see a cop pass behind the bank. So in the fall of that year, when it got dark early, I think either a Thursday or a Friday night, we came back.

We drove a stolen car. Stealing cars was actually pretty easy in those days. In the 1950s, if you owned a G.M. automobile and you lost your car keys, you'd call a G.M. dealer, who would come with a ring of about sixty car keys. Each key on the ring had a number stamped on it. The G.M. dealer would sit in your car, trying key after key in the ignition until he found the right key. Then, he would set the key cutting machine to the number from that key. Once we learned about this, we knew all we had to do was steal one of those rings. We could just take ten keys off of that ring and find a car to steal real fast. Sometimes you had to wiggle the key a little, but one of those keys would always work.

We parked the stolen car right in back of the bank. Just after the bank locked its front door, my brother and I came in the back. We were both a little scared, but we both had big balls. After the robbery, we left through the back door and got into our hot car. We drove across the Ohio River Bridge, back into Steubenville, and back to our car, which we had parked at the railroad station across from the Venetian Gardens. We were elated with our success. We went into Venetian's and dined on spaghetti and meatballs. We couldn't believe how easy it was to rob a bank. And no one but my brother and I knew that we had done it.

If we knew then what we found out through experience later, we would have robbed that bank in the morning hours after the armored truck dropped off the money for the steel workers' paychecks. Live and learn—and learn we did.

Robbing banks was our preferred method of generating income for a couple years. That changed one day when I was dropping off my sister for her shift at Isaly's, a local dairy and restaurant. As I sat in the parking lot of the shopping plaza in Boardman, Ohio, I watched one of the employees inside the bank next to Isaly's. I was captivated as I watched him pull bag after bag of money out of the bank's night deposit safe. I knew right then that my brother and I needed to get into bank safes at night to score the really big money.

Thanks to the Diebold Company, becoming sophisticated bank burglars was a relatively easy feat for us. As I waited for my sister that morning, I noticed a sticker in the window of the bank stating that the bank was protected by Diebold. Obviously, what we had to do was make a late night visit to Diebold.

We used an ordinary telephone book to locate Diebold in Canton, Ohio. My brother and I went there several nights in a row and just watched. We watched to see who came and went and what security measures they used. It was a large plant with several buildings surrounded by a fence. At the main entrance, there was a security guard, but he never once left his shanty. When we were confident no one would catch us on the premises, we jumped the fence and began checking the doors of the buildings. Almost immediately, we found an unlocked door, and when we walked in, my brother and I knew we struck gold.

The building was filled with safes in all stages of assembly. We saw several large, round safe doors. We loaded a safe door weighing approximately three hundred pounds onto a two-wheeled cart and took the door home with us. It didn't take us very long to learn the mechanics of the safe door, and we developed a "jig" for the specific purpose of drilling into bank safes. (See jig, page 154.)

The next step in our education was figuring out how to beat the silent alarm systems used by banks. Of course, the logical way to learn that was to make a trip back to Diebold. With the company's security guard again safely in his shanty, my brother and I, again, hopped Diebold's fence and began our hunt for an alarm system.

Within minutes, we struck gold again at Diebold. Armed with a flashlight, I looked through a window of a locked building and noticed what appeared to be an alarm mounted to a three by four piece of plywood. I pried open the window and we quickly discovered that an alarm was, in fact, mounted to that piece of plywood, and that it was an alarm used to train Diebold's employees. That night, we left Diebold with the alarm, several books on troubleshooting alarms, and the blueprints of the alarm's wiring circuits.

When we examined our finds in my brother's garage, we discovered that Diebold had provided us with an entire alarm system, complete with the alarm's main control module that would be mounted in a bank vault; two wires leading to an alarm-receiving module that would be used at a police station and would light up in the event of an alarm drop at a bank; and wires leading from the main module to a contact and a heat sensor that would be in a bank's night deposit safe. With the unwitting help of Diebold, we almost were to our goal.

The only thing left for us to do was to figure out how to beat the alarm's electrical system. My brother visited his friend, Jack, who was a genius in the area of electronics. Jack discovered that the alarm ran on a direct current (DC), and that a number of pulses were transmitted over the two wires from the alarm's main module inside the vault to the receiving module at the police station. Within a week, Jack developed our best friend, an alarm bypass box that we named "The Boss Man." (See diagram, page 155.)

I like the way I am. I like to steal money from banks. Those bastards hurt so many poor people by foreclosing on peoples' homes and repossessing their cars. Yes, I feel sorry for stealing from people's safety deposit boxes, but when I'm in a vault punching out safety deposit locks and looking through the goods, I really can't tell the rich from the poor. I just have to take whatever I think can make me money.

For several years, my brother and I, along with The Boss Man, traveled throughout the United States beating bank vaults and drilling into night deposit safes. Life couldn't have been better, and James and I thought we were invincible.

And then, one fateful night in 1971, I got a score from Jimmy Hoffa.

Chapter Two

The Score

When all the excitement started, I was living with my family in Boardman, Ohio, a sleepy suburb south of Youngstown. I couldn't have been happier, and had no idea what was coming my way. I had a beautiful wife named Linda and two adorable little girls, Melissa and Amie-Jo. My mother-in-law, Mary Mulligan, was also living with us at the time. We were getting on like any normal family, enjoying the pleasures of suburban life.

I had another life under the surface, though. By 1972, I was already known as one of the best bank burglars in the country. That's an important distinction, by the way: burglar, not robber. A robber goes in at gunpoint and robs a bank while people are inside it. What I did was much more difficult.

My modus operandi was defeating bank alarms, then either blasting a hole in the concrete vault or drilling into night-deposit safes. Once inside the vault, I would punch out the locks from the safety deposit boxes and relieve them of their valuables. Cash, jewelry, bonds—anything that could be easily sold, I took.

Of course, I didn't do all of this alone. My brother James was the explosives expert. He could blow a hole in a vault so quietly even the building's neighbors would have no idea what was going on inside. My brother-in-law, Chuck, was also on my crew. He usually handled the getaway car and other details.

As you can tell, the crimes we pulled were far from simple smash-and-grab jobs. We were highly skilled professionals—and we took a lot of pride in our work. Sure, we were criminals, but we were damn good criminals, and usually no one got hurt. Moreover, it was how we made a living. In Youngstown, the steel industry was starting to die out, and it was getting harder and harder to make money honestly. So we did what we had to do, and did it well.

Bank robbing wasn't my only source of income. I also owned a coal mining company with James called the Dinsio Brothers Mining Company, which was located in Salem, Ohio. Every Thursday afternoon, I would drive to nearby Cleveland to see my friend, Butchie Cisterino. Butchie ran a barbotte—a gambling dice game—for the Little Italy mob just off of Mayfield Road. I was a partner on the operation, receiving 10 percent of the game's profit, which I'd go pick up every Thursday—a lucky thing too, because it was on one of those Thursdays that I heard about the score of a lifetime.

On a Thursday evening in January, I arrived in Little Italy and squeezed down the long, narrow alley to the old house where the game was held. Mo the doorman let me inside, where I found Butchie taking care of some business for the game. As he worked, he turned to me and said the words that would change my life: "I think I have a score you might be interested in."

"Oh yeah?" I said.

Butchie nodded. "Let's grab a sandwich, and I'll run it down for you."

We left the game and went up the street to a little Italian restaurant. But we weren't the only people there. Also at the restaurant was John Scalish, a boss with the Cleveland mob, along with one of his underbosses, Jack White. Scalish wielded a great deal of power for the mafia, both in Cleveland and around the country. I knew that he and Jack were responsible for a lot of broken bones on orders from the mob and their political arm, the Teamsters Union. They weren't the type of guys you wanted to mess with.

Scalish and Jack stopped to talk to us for a minute, asking me how business was going. I told them that everything was fine, and Scalish seemed pleased. Then he asked if they could have a word with Butchie privately. Leaving them alone, I went to sit at another table in the restaurant and watched as the three men discussed business. The coincidence of running into Scalish and Jack seemed too great. I started to think that maybe Butchie's "score" was a job for the mafia—something I promised my father I would never do.

After talking for a few minutes, Scalish and Jack left, and Butchie returned to our table. We ordered a couple of sandwiches. I waited for Butchie to get around to talking about the job.

Finally, he spoke up. "How would you like to steal a few million dollars from Tricky Dick?"

"Who?" I asked. I had no idea what he was talking about.

"Tricky Dick. You know, President Nixon." In 1972, Richard Nixon was still in the White House. Watergate was still months away. However, he had already gained a reputation for wheeling and dealing, and the nickname "Tricky Dick" had stuck.

I looked at Butchie. I couldn't tell if he was serious. "And how would we do that?"

Butchie went on to tell me that a mutual friend, BB—a representative with the Teamsters Union in Cleveland—was currently in Detroit. A friend of his there had told him that Nixon, along with John Connally, the former governor of Texas, had been shaking down the U.S. Dairy Farmers for a lot of cash.

Nixon had promised to ensure that the price of raw milk would be raised if the dairy farmers' lobby gave a big contribution to his reelection campaign. According to BB's friend, the majority of that money was stashed away in a safety deposit box, along with other cash and valuables the President had acquired through underhanded dealings.

The total haul, Butchie claimed, was thirty million dollars or more.

I gaped at him. It seemed impossible. "Do you really believe that?" I couldn't help but ask. The idea that the President of the United States would store stolen money—*thirty million* of it—in a safety deposit box seemed completely ridiculous. Too ridiculous. It sounded like an FBI trap.

Butchie just shrugged. "I can only tell you what I've been told. It might be true. Everyone in this country knows the government crooks in Washington D.C. deal with big bucks and steal like mad. It's just that they very seldom ever get caught doing it."

Butchie had a point, but I still wasn't sold. I needed more details. "Where's the bank? In D.C., near the White House?"

"I'm not sure. But if you want me to, I'll go see BB and get some more information on it. You want to come along?"

I said no—he could handle BB on his own. But I wanted to know who was giving out the score. The last thing I needed was to get set up by the FBI.

"From what BB has already told me, it comes from a good source with the Teamsters in Detroit," Butchie said. "I'll let you know what he says after I talk to him."

It didn't seem like there would be any harm in getting more details, so I told Butchie to find out where the bank was located. If it was in a good location and I could find out how to beat the vault without getting caught, I would get my brother and we could check it out for ourselves.

After Butchie and I split up, I decided to stay in Cleveland overnight and visit my friend Deacon. Deacon worked as a professional booster—i.e., shoplifter. If it wasn't nailed down, Deacon could lift it. He had everything from fine furs to nice men's suits to ladies' clothing. I wanted to pick up a white mink for my wife, and while I was at it, I'd see if anything else Deacon was selling caught my eye.

I called Deacon and arranged to meet him at a local Holiday Inn. When I got there, Deacon hadn't arrived yet. I bought a cup of coffee and waited. As I sat there, I started to go through everything that Butchie had told me. Thirty million dollars was a lot of money, but it all sounded too much like an FBI setup. Besides, one million C-notes—slang for hundred dollar bills—weighed just over twenty pounds. Thirty times that would be over six hundred pounds of loot. Nixon would have to have a pretty big safety deposit box to hold that, and that could create some difficult logistics.

I waited for Deacon for half an hour, but he never showed. When I called him, he claimed something had come up and asked if we could meet the next day instead. I was ticked off at the delay but agreed. I wanted to get that mink!

Checking into the motel, I lay on the bed and stared up at the ceiling. My mind drifted to a sweet thought: maybe Butchie's score could actually be legit.

Thirty million dollars.

That was a lot to pass up on the chance that the score was a setup.

Friday morning, I got up, got dressed, and headed back to the old house where the gambling game was being held. Butchie wasn't around, so I caught up with Mo the doorman. Around noon, Butchie showed up. He had just finished talking with BB, who was heading to Detroit for a Teamsters meeting. BB said he would find out more about the score.

"Okay," I said. "We'll just have to wait and see what BB has to say." We decided we would meet up again the following Thursday when I came back to Cleveland for the game.

After that, I left and met up with Deacon, who had several full-length mink coats, some mink stoles, chinchilla furs, and mink hats—all hot off the hangers of a department store in Akron, Ohio. I bought a white mink stole for my wife, and Deacon threw in a mink hat and some perfume. Some guys bring home flowers after a business trip; in my line of work, Linda got hot furs. I loved being able to make her smile.

With my shopping done, I got on the turnpike and headed home. As the miles went by, I kept thinking about that thirty million. I couldn't help fantasize that it might all be real—and to start thinking of what my plan might be. The bank's alarm system probably wouldn't be a problem; I had yet to meet a system I couldn't beat. Nearly every bank in the United States used a Diebold or Mosler alarm at that time, and I had tackled every model those companies made.

As soon as I got off the turnpike, I called my brother James and told him to meet me at a beer lounge out in the suburbs. When I told him about Butchie's score, he had the same doubts I did.

"Do you believe it's possible?" he asked. "Thirty million dollars is a lot of money."

"Yeah, it is," I said. "And I think it could very well be possible. After all, those big shots running the country deal with that kind of cash every day."

James still looked skeptical. "Stop and think about it," I said. "If you and I were running the country and we had a chance to steal big time cash like they do, we'd be stealing billions instead of millions—and we wouldn't have to shake down the poor dairy farmers to do it. You know why thieves like Nixon and Connally have to shake down people? Because they're not like us; they don't have the guts to just go and steal it honestly."

My brother nodded in agreement. "When will we know more about the deal?"

"I'm meeting with Butchie next week. Hopefully, we'll have some information after that."

My brother looked me in the eye. "And what about Butchie?" he asked. "Do you really think he's legit? I know you two are close, but are you sure about this one? Those feds would do anything to see our bodies dead in some bank vault."

I knew the feds would love to get their hands on us, but I trusted Butchie. Besides, I just knew that deep down, those agents who walked into a burglarized bank vault all wished they were us. They wished they had the balls to pull off the kind of things we did. They're all petty thieves at heart.

If only I had known how petty and thieving they could get.

"Look," I told my brother, "If it doesn't feel right, we can pass. Let's just wait and see what Butchie brings back. If the facts sound good, we can go take a look-see ourselves."

The following Thursday, I was back in Cleveland, talking with Butchie. To this day, I'll never forget his first words to me: "Amil, you won't believe this. Jimmy Hoffa is the one giving out the score."

He was right—I couldn't believe it. But it seemed to be true. Jimmy Hoffa was the head of the Teamsters Union and in tight with the Italian mafia. He'd been doing time in prison but was now out on parole. It turned out that Nixon had actually commuted Hoffa's sentence in order to get him out early—a favor that had cost Hoffa three million dollars. Now it looked like Hoffa was trying to get his money back, along with an extra twenty-seven million.

"We have to keep this quiet," Butchie said. I knew he was right. There was no way Hoffa would want information like this getting out. Butchie still hadn't found out where the bank was located, but promised to talk to BB and get back to me. A week later, he told me the location: the United California Bank, located at 6 Monarch Bay Shopping Center in ... Laguna Niguel, California.

Laguna Niguel? Where the hell was that?

I had assumed the bank would be in Washington D.C., or possibly Virginia—somewhere the President could keep an eye on it. But California?

We looked up Laguna Niguel on the map and found it was in Orange County. It started to make sense: the bank was right near Nixon's home in San Clemente. Using that bank, Nixon could keep the money away from anyone in Washington but still have it someplace familiar and close at hand. Suddenly, this score was starting to look a lot more legit.

But that was nothing compared to the next bit of information from Butchie: apparently, BB could give us the numbers of the actual safety deposit boxes that held Nixon's money. *Someone must really have it in for the President*, I thought. And the person who was hiding the money for him had to be involved. After all, it's not like Nixon would carry all of that money into the bank himself, and who else would know those box numbers?

California was a far cry from Youngstown, Ohio. But this new information made the score seem even more definite. I decided it was worth checking out the bank in person.

Chapter Three

Westward Bound

Upon arriving home from Cleveland, I met with my brother and my brother-in-law, Chuck, to update them on the new info from Butchie. They agreed that all three of us should go size up the bank.

Besides being an expert in handling explosives, my brother was also strong as an ox. Chuck, meanwhile, was great on the walkie-talkie as a lookout. Both were good men, and I was lucky to have such a solid crew. Together, we had beaten quite a few banks without any major problems.

We decided to drive to California the next day. I sent Chuck to pick up the blow car—a vehicle registered to a bogus name and address that couldn't be associated with any of us. We packed up our suitcases, along with a pair of binoculars, three walkie-talkies, two portable hand-held police scanners, a set of lock picks, a volt-ohm meter, and a small amplifier that would allow us to listen to an alarm system on telephone lines—you know, the usual.

Early the next morning, we were on our way. We had a long ride ahead of us, and during the drive, we talked through everything about the score—the burglar's dream of a thirty million dollar haul, what Nixon was doing with the money, the bank, the location of the bank, everything around the location of the bank.

My brother thought it might be a good idea to rent a car in Las Vegas. That way we'd have a ride with Nevada or California plates that would blend in better in the area around the bank. I agreed about the license plate but had a better idea than renting: our friend Joey, who lived in Vegas. I figured, when we hit Nevada, we could give him a call and ask to borrow his car for a few days. Joey was a good guy. He wouldn't tell anyone that we'd been through town.

When we arrived in Las Vegas—a town I love, by the way!—I met with Joey and asked him about the car. He was more than happy to lend it to me, but on one condition: that I tell him whether or not I was planning a job.

"Hell, no!" I said. "You know me better than that. I'd never borrow your car to commit a crime." I may have liked Joey, but this was too big of a score to risk a lot of people knowing about it. Instead, I told him I was looking for someone who owed me money, and if the guy saw a car with Ohio plates following him, he'd probably run.

So Joey let us use his old Ford, and after stopping to fill up the gas tank, check the tires, and buy some maps, we were on our way to California. We arrived at the Laguna Niguel shopping center around four in the afternoon, and the first business we spotted was our target—the United California Bank.

"There she sits, boys," I said.

We couldn't have asked for a better location. The shopping center was perched above the Pacific Coast Highway, up on a hill with not much else around it. I could immediately tell that blowing a hole in the vault would be a snap. With no houses or 24/7 businesses nearby, there was little chance the sound of a small explosion would be heard.

"If Nixon really is hiding his money in this bank, he's crazy and sure as hell shouldn't be the President of the United States!" my brother remarked as we looked at the isolated building. Chuck and I both agreed. We counted six big parking lot lights, and only one entrance to the plaza's parking lot—another mark in our favor. Even better, the area looked like a wealthy one, which meant that the other safety deposit boxes in the vault would likely have some pretty valuable things stashed in them as well.

We decided to watch the bank that night and scope out what happened around the shopping center after the parking lot lights went off. The shopping center also included a supermarket and, towards the far end, a bar. Even if the supermarket had stock boys working through the night, the bank was far enough away from the store that no one would be able to hear dynamite exploding. There was also a drug store directly next to the bank, but we were sure it wouldn't stay open all night.

It was perfect.

To the left of the bank, up a long hillside covered with thick brush, we saw a car moving along a small road. I told Chuck to follow that street, Crown Valley Parkway. At the top of the road, we found that we could see the entire shopping center and the roofs of the stores—including that of the bank. The building had a big air conditioning unit on its roof. I realized I could tap into the power lines of that unit in order to pick up the electricity we needed to operate our tools. The setup was looking better and better.

A little farther up the road, we found a sandy half-circle parking area offering a picturesque view of the valley. Looking down on the shopping center, the bank resembled a sitting duck. A dead duck, in fact, just waiting to be plucked.

We decided that night my brother and I would lay and watch the area around the bank, see what happened around there. Chuck wanted to park the car someplace so all three of us could stay at the bank, but I shot that idea down. Someone might notice the car parked and take down the tag number. Instead, I told Chuck to find a place to lay low. The following night, he and I would lie on the bank. After some discussion, we decided it would be best to spend all weekend watching the bank, in order to figure out what the usual schedule was—and especially to see if there was a cleaning crew that came in at night.

We had a few hours to kill until dark, so we drove down the Pacific Coast Highway and found a restaurant that served something other than hamburgers—our only source of food while making the drive out from Ohio!

"Do you really think there's thirty million dollars in that vault?" my brother asked as we ate.

"I'll tell you what," I said. "If Jimmy Hoffa is giving out this information, it's probably pretty accurate."

"Nixon and Connally," my brother said, shaking his head. "They're both crooks." He gave a chuckle. "They stole from the people and now we're stealing from them. The Lord works in mysterious ways." Chuck and I both burst out laughing. You had to admit, there did seem to be some justice in what we were doing!

As we finished our meal, we discussed our plans for the evening. We decided that Chuck could use his blow driver's license to rent a motel room thirty miles or so from the area. After he dropped us off near the bank, we'd stay in touch over walkie-talkie, and if all went as planned, he'd pick us up the following morning at five.

Chuck let us out of the car on the Coast Highway around ten thirty that night. The drugstore was still open, as was the bar, but the supermarket looked closed.

I turned on my walkie-talkie to talk to Chuck. "Keep your radio on," I told him. "Check in with me every mile. Let's see what kind of range we can get on these things." The walkie-talkies had been expensive—three thousand dollars apiece. That money certainly seemed worth it when we discovered we could get a good seven or eight mile range on them! Moreover, the frequency the radios operated on was under channel one—the same frequency assigned to the United States Secret Service. That meant we could talk on the radio and never have to worry about anyone busting in on our conversation.

After Chuck let us out, we made our way up the hill, struggling through the heavy brush until we reached the side across from the bank. From there, we could see the front door and the blacktop entrance leading into the plaza. I scanned the parking lot through our binoculars. Nothing was moving.

Then, after about ten minutes, a cleaning crew arrived and headed into the bank. While they were inside working, my brother snuck closer to the building to look inside. "I can see the crew dusting the teller's stations," his voice crackled over the walkie-talkie. "And there she is, in the back left corner—the big, stainless steel bank vault door!"

"Good," I radioed back. "We'll take care of the door later."

There were several reasons we usually never attempted to go through a vault door. First of all, a concrete bank vault is usually easy enough to blast into—so why bother with the door? Second, burglaries were most likely to be discovered by a cleaning crew walking right in on you while you were trying to make a hole in the vault door! Better to avoid that possibility. Third, if you were actually lucky enough to make a hole in the door big enough to get through, you would only have a limited period of time that night to clean out the bank's money and safety deposit boxes. The minute someone entered the bank in the morning—whether it was a cleaning crew or an ambitious bank employee doing some work over the weekend—it would be obvious that the vault had been breached. All in all, going through the vault door was way more trouble than it was worth.

After the cleaning crew left, I told my brother to walk up to the door and see if there was an alarm sticker giving the name of the company protecting the bank. "Nada," my brother reported back. In fact, the only signs painted on the door were the business hours and a notice that the bank was closed on Saturdays. Next, my brother checked out the door lock cylinder to find the name of the manufacturer. Luck was on our side again: it turned out to be a simple mechanism that would be easy to pick.

As my brother reported all of this to me over the walkie-talkie, all I could think was, *Why would the President of the United States be hiding money in such an insecure bank?* The only reason I could think of was to fool his political cronies—or thieves like me! No one would suspect the President would be stupid enough to keep his money in such a flimsy bank sitting in this little shopping center.

When my brother came back to where I was waiting, we decided I should go ahead and pick the door lock, go inside the bank, and see if I could locate the telephone line junction box. That would let me read the wires of the bank's alarm system, which would tell us exactly what kind of alarm we'd be trying to beat.

I was preparing to take my alarm testing meter and amplifier out of my small camouflage carrying bag when a car turned into the shopping center. It stopped at the cement curb just over to the left side of the bank. As my brother and I took cover, a tall, thin man got out. He was followed seconds later by a black German shepherd, who jumped out after him. My brother and I watched anxiously, waiting to see if the man headed into the bank. But the man just stood by his car while the dog lifted its leg over some flowers along the concrete sidewalk.

Then the dog started walking down the sidewalk in front of the bank, moving at a quick pace past the front doors of the other stores. While the man lit a cigarette and continued to wait by the car, the dog circled the shopping center. It seemed to be patrolling the area all by itself. I watched the dog through my binoculars until it disappeared around the corner of the supermarket.

My brother and I kept as still as possible in the heavy brush. We were no more than a hundred feet from the man. Finally, a minute or so later, the dog rounded the corner by the front of the bank. Lifting its leg on the flowers one more time, it headed back to the car. The man opened the car door, the dog jumped in, and they both drove away.

Sitting in the bushes, my brother and I just stared at each other. "Do you believe that?" my brother said. We had never seen a dog patrolman before! But at least now we knew we had to keep our eyes open for him. We didn't know whether the man and his dog would be back or if they made regular rounds, but we knew that dogs have good noses. If this one caught our scent anywhere near the bank, our entire operation could be finished.

We decided that the best thing to do would be to watch the bank from a distance for the rest of the night and see if the patrol dog made a return appearance. While we were waiting, I went behind the bank and tried to locate a telephone line junction box with the phone line wires going directly into the bank. You see, it's not only voltage on burglar alarm wires; there can also be what is called "line security" running on the same wires to stop a burglar from just hooking a battery on the alarm wires. I had to find the pair of telephone line wires carrying the silent alarm heading to the police and read them with my meter to determine what specific alarm we had to beat.

With my walkie-talkie in hand, I took my ohmmeter and amplifier and walked around to the back of the building. Just above the bank's back door was a small dim light. I looked up and saw a Diebold alarm bell mounted on the wall about twenty feet up. "Yes!" I whispered to myself. I couldn't have asked for anything better. I had tackled everything Diebold had created, and I was sure this alarm would be no problem.

Still, I knew from years of experience that just because a Diebold bell was hanging on a bank, it didn't necessarily mean that the bank's alarm protection was provided by Diebold. I'd been on jobs before where we'd assumed the system was Diebold because of the alarm bell, only to get into the phone junction box and discover that we were dealing with a completely different alarm system. I didn't want any surprises on this job, so I knew I had to find the telephone line junction box. That way, I could read the alarm wires and make sure it was a Diebold system.

I looked around behind the bank and along the backs of the other stores, but there was no sign of a telephone line junction box. That wasn't too unusual. Sometimes the main telephone cable line runs down through the steel joists over the top of the stores in a plaza, and the phone company will just branch off a few pairs of phone line wires and install a telephone junction box in a store's utility room. I figured I'd just have to pick the lock on the bank's front door and go inside to find the alarm.

With a plan in mind, I made my way back to where my brother was waiting and told him everything I had seen. We both wanted to make sure the man and his dog weren't coming back, so we decided I would wait until the following night to pick the lock on the front door.

Around three o'clock, the bar closed. Everything was dead. We didn't see a single police car, and very few calls came over the scanner. It looked like Laguna Niguel was a pretty sleepy place.

Seeing that there wasn't much action, I decided to take a walk along the parking lot to the far end of the supermarket and get a better idea of the area. "Keep an eye out for cars, or any pedestrians that might come into the parking lot," I told my brother. Then I set off. As I reached the other side of the lot, I noticed a worn path just to the left of the supermarket. It looked like it was used regularly, so I figured I'd check it out.

After walking about eight hundred feet or so up a small grade, I noticed a complex of lights in the distance that looked like apartments. Guessing that the path led right to them, I followed the trail, which also led past a golf course. My hunch proved to be right. Seeing how convenient the location was, I thought we could rent one of the apartments and use it as our base of operations. With the walking path and line of sight to the shopping center, it would be the perfect place.

Making my way back down the path, I met up with my brother again and told him about the apartments. We'd have to keep an eye out for any pedestrians on the path, but it seemed like a quiet enough trail.

At five o'clock, Chuck called over the radio and asked if we were ready to go. "Give us ten minutes," I told him. We headed back to the parkway, where Chuck picked us up. He had rented a motel room thirty miles away. During the drive, my brother and I told him about the cleaning crew and patrol dog. By the time we made it to the motel, we were exhausted. We threw ourselves onto the beds and slept.

It was late afternoon when we woke up. We headed out for some food, then made our way back to the bank to have another look around. I especially wanted to check out the apartments I had spotted from the trail.

As we drove around, Laguna Niguel started to look better and better. Late-model expensive cars cruised the streets, and all the homes and high-end condos were well-kept. The area was definitely a wealthy one. I had Chuck drive over to the apartments. Upon arrival, we discovered that they were actually condos. We got the name and phone number of the leasing agent, but Chuck and my brother were worried that the location was too close to our target. I reassured them that it was no problem—no one would even know we had been there.

Looking back on that conversation, I wish I had listened to Chuck and my brother. Maybe it wouldn't have made a difference in the end, but at least the Feds' job would have been harder.

The area around the shopping center wasn't big, and after checking out the condos, we still had time to kill before we could safely return and stake out the bank for the night. We ended up driving down the Pacific Coast Highway to San Clemente, where President Nixon had his house. I didn't think much of the town, and we soon headed back to the motel room to get ready for that night.

The plan was for Chuck and I to watch the bank just as my brother and I had done the previous night. If things looked good, I would go inside and locate the telephone junction box, so that I could figure out what kind of an alarm we were dealing with.

My brother dropped Chuck and I off. Shortly after we installed ourselves on the hill, the bank's cleaning crew arrived. They did their jobs and left, but I was still worried about the man with the dog showing up. Chuck and I waited. And waited. Finally, I figured the dog wasn't coming.

"I'm heading into the bank," I told Chuck.

Chuck wasn't keen on the idea. "We better wait," he cautioned.

"It's getting too late," I insisted. "If I'm going to do it, I have to go now. Besides, I don't think that dog is coming."

I was just about to approach the bank's front doors when Chuck said he could see a couple walking down the entrance to the shopping center's plaza. They had a dog with them, but I could see through the binoculars that the dog was a poodle, and I didn't recognize the man as the one who had been there with the German shepherd the previous night. The couple walked down the sidewalk, past the front door of the stores. It really just looked like they were walking their dog. After they walked by the supermarket, Chuck and I didn't see them again. We figured they had taken the path up to the condos. We were in the clear.

Finally set to go, I put my earpiece in and had Chuck turn on his walkie-talkie. I headed across the blacktop to the bank's front door. Before doing anything with the lock, I peeked through the window, trying to see through the dim lighting in the lobby whether there were any alarmed motion detectors on the walls. I didn't see any, so I put my penlight between my teeth and focused the light beam on the door lock. In less than a minute, I had the lock picked. I was in.

Once inside the bank, I went down the hallway leading to the back door. I wanted to make sure I could open it quickly if I needed to beat a fast retreat. Sure enough, the back door opened easily. Certain that I would have an escape route if things went bad, I went into the utility room. The telephone junction box wasn't there. I knew it had to be somewhere in the bank, so I headed back to the lobby. Making my way down the hallway, I spotted a small plywood door with a long handle. I opened it, and there it was: the telephone junction box.

The first things to catch my eye were two red plastic caps covering brass terminal posts. *Gotcha!* I thought. I knew the bank's alarm system wires would be connected to those brass terminals. It was so obvious; it was almost as if the alarm was telling me, "Here I am!"

In all my years of beating alarm systems, I've found that in nearly every instance, an alarm company will red cap the alarm terminals in the telephone line junction box. If they don't do that, they will tie a white tag around the two alarm wires saying—I kid you not—"Alarm. Do not remove."

They make it that easy.

With my goal in sight, I took my volt-ohm meter and set it to read DC voltage—the current a Diebold system would be operating on. In general, the Diebold system works by sending voltage, or voltage and a specific number of pulses per second, over the alarm wires. These would go to a receiving module at either a commercial alarm monitoring company or directly to the police station. The pulses are generated in the alarm's main control panel, which is located and locked in the bank's vault. I removed the two red caps and held one meter probe to each of the brass terminals. To my surprise, the meter showed no voltage reading.

Very strange, I thought. I knew that wasn't right for a Diebold alarm. I set the meter to read AC voltage and touched one probe to a terminal and the other to an earth ground in the telephone junction box in order to check the other possible systems it could be. Still no voltage reading. I reversed the probe and did the same—no voltage reading.

That information eliminated the possibility of an AC alarm system. The lack of voltage meant I was probably dealing with a circuit alarm system, but I wanted to make sure. I set my meter to read for ohms, and sure enough, it was a circuit alarm. I could hardly believe it. A circuit alarm is one of the worst alarms on the market. It was the easiest to bypass, and the last thing you would want protecting your valuables. It certainly wasn't adequate for a whole bank filled with valuables—not against a thief like me.

It was too easy. I never like it when things are too easy. I started to think that maybe the bank also had an Automatic Telephone Dialer alarm as a backup for the circuit alarm. If there were, I figured I could take care of it when we came back to beat the vault. All I would have to do would be to disconnect one phone line wire on each set of brass terminals. If we got into the vault and found there was no telephone dialer control panel, then great. If there was, I could just disable it so it wouldn't be capable of calling out. Then I would go back and reconnect the telephone wires I had disconnected on the terminals. That way, if someone came into the bank and wanted to use the phone while we were in the vault, they would have no idea that something was up.

I replaced the two red caps on the brass terminals and shut the plywood door. Since I was inside the bank, I figured I should also take a look at the top of the vault to see what we might be facing up there. Going back to the utility room, I found a ladder and carried it to a small room off the main hallway, setting it down alongside the wall of the vault. Climbing the ladder, I lifted a ceiling tile to get a look at the crawl space between the bank's ceiling and the roof. I could see the roof was made of plywood. It appeared to be six or seven feet up from the top of the vault. That would give us plenty of room to work. I replaced the ceiling tile and took the ladder back to the utility room.

As I was leaving, I spotted a small fridge and, opening it up, found some sodas. I grabbed two—burglary is thirsty work!—before heading out of the bank and locking the front door behind me.

As Chuck and I sat drinking our sodas, I told him about the circuit alarm.

"You're kidding me, right?" He was just as amazed as I was. I warned him there might be a backup Automated Telephone Dialer alarm, but it shouldn't be a problem. When I told him about my plans for the phone system, Chuck was impressed.

"You're a thinker," he said. "Do whatever you have to so we get that money."

Sitting in the brush overlooking the bank, I started to think over everything we had learned since coming to California. The quiet location, wealthy neighborhood, huge haul, and poor security system all combined to create the perfect job. I just hoped that Hoffa wasn't playing a game with us.

Thinking over the timing of the burglary, I realized we could pull it off over a weekend. The bank would be closed, and that would give us three nights inside the vault. Turning to Chuck, I outlined the plan:

We would make a large hole in the plywood roof over the vault on Thursday night. We'd bring along our tools, as well as sandbags, which we would use to muffle the sound of the dynamite set in the crawl space between the underside of the roof and the top of the vault. Then we'd seal the hole so that no one would be able to spot it unless they did a thorough check of the roof. Moreover, if it rained, no water would leak in and alert the bank employees to the breach. Then, on Friday night, I'd take care of the alarm system and my brother would blast the vault. We'd hit Nixon's boxes first, of course. However, we would still have all night on Saturday and Sunday to loot the other safety deposit boxes.

Chuck and I kept an eye on the bank for the rest of the night, but no one—not even the patrolling German shepherd—showed up. At five o'clock, Chuck and I made our way back to the parkway, where my brother picked us up. I immediately told my brother about the circuit alarm.

"Are they crazy?" was all he could say. When I told him about the space above the vault, along with the fact that the roof was made out of plywood, he was even more surprised. "Good," he said. "We'll use a saw to cut the hole in the roof and tar to seal the hole so no rain leaks in." I had to smile—my brother and I always think alike.

On Friday we rested. In the evening, Chuck dropped my brother and me off on the parkway. We made our way to the bank and spread out our tarp, ready for another night of watching our target. Very little was coming over the police scanner, and the cleaning crew came and went. Once again, there was no German shepherd. Saturday and Sunday nights were pretty much the same, which told us what we needed to know: there wouldn't be any weekend surprises during the job.

On Monday, we got a few hours of sleep before checking out of the motel. We drove to Las Vegas to return Joey's car, then picked up our blow car and headed back to Ohio. I was convinced the job was legit—or at least legit enough to warrant the risk.

It was time to start prepping.

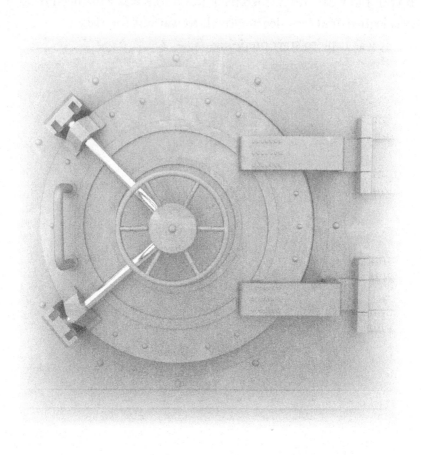

Chapter Four

Prep Time

Besides being an explosives expert, my brother is a skilled designer of burglary tools. When we got back to Ohio, I told him what we needed for the job. One of the most important pieces of equipment was a drill motor that ran silently, because we didn't want anyone to hear us drilling through the cement. My brother immediately got to work on the job. I sent Chuck to our farm to pick up our acetylene-cutting torch and make sure it still ran properly. Whenever we planned a score, I worked my ass off to make sure we had the tools to get the job done right. I had no idea what kind of safe we would face inside the vault. I wanted to make sure we had everything we could possibly need.

Federal laws require that the entirety of a bank's operating cash—the money they have on hand—be secured under two timed locks. The bank's main vault door has the first timer, and either a safe or a heavy-duty steel cabinet in the bank's vault has the second one, which must have a fifteen-minute delayed timer. The delay discourages bank robbers from getting to the inner safe. If they've just invaded the bank and cleaned out the tellers' drawers and held up everyone at gunpoint, they're going to be itching to leave, believe me. There's no way in hell anyone is going to stand around for fifteen minutes waiting for the timer to run out.

But not all banks follow the regulations. I've come across my fair share of safes and cabinets without timers. Some I could even open with a screwdriver. But I didn't want to assume this vault would be that easy. Too much confidence can be deadly. So, not knowing what kind of a safe we'd find, I told Chuck to pack a couple of air tanks for the acetylene torch. If we came up against a tough safe, we would have to cut it open.

Once I had my brother and Chuck working on our tools, I went to Cleveland to see Butchie. I wanted to give him a rundown on what we had learned in California and let him know that we were taking the job. He met me at the Dew Drop Inn, a massage parlor he operated just off of the turnpike. I told him we could beat the bank without a problem. I just hoped the money would be there.

"It's there," he insisted. "Believe me." Then he filled me in on the details. Apparently, the money was a portion of a payoff Nixon had received from a man in Florida. The man was also holding millions of the President's dollars at his own bank in the Sunshine State. Butchie asked if I ever wondered what would happen if Nixon found out I was involved with the theft of his money.

I hadn't given the idea much thought. The way I saw it, Nixon got the money from extorting poor dairy farmers and doing underhanded favors for others. What could he tell his FBI director? Find those dirty bastards that stole my money? No way. The asshole wouldn't like it, but he'd have to take the loss.

"That's life," I said. "If you like the ups, you have to take the downs when they come your way."

Butchie just laughed.

Knowing that Hoffa had paid Nixon three million dollars to commute his sentence, my next question to Butchie was all business. "How much does Hoffa want for giving out the score?"

"I don't know," Butchie said. "But BB's friend in Detroit thinks we should give him the three million he paid Nixon."

I didn't think Hoffa had actually paid three million dollars. That was just him talking big. But three million for the score seemed fair if thirty million was actually in the vault. The truth was, though, we really didn't know anything going into this. In case the estimate was low, I knew we should settle on a percentage now. The last thing I wanted was to haggle over cuts once the job was done, especially since Hoffa had a brutal reputation.

"If Hoffa thinks we screwed him, there won't be anywhere we can hide."

Butchie nodded. "What do you think is fair?"

"Find out if Hoffa will agree to five percent of what we take out of Nixon's safety deposit boxes. But only what's in Tricky Dick's boxes counts. Anything else we grab is a bonus for my crew." Butchie agreed to pass along the message. He said he would also try to find out the exact numbers for Nixon's safety deposit boxes so we could find them easily in the vault.

With our business done, I got back on the turnpike and headed home. As the highway raced by, my mind couldn't relax. I was still worried the job might be an FBI trap. An FBI agent had once told a deputy sheriff friend of mine that the government was dying to catch me in a bank vault. If that day ever came, the agent said I would be coming out in a body bag. That kind of talk sticks in your mind. But warnings like that never stopped me from going after a new job. They just made me more careful.

I knew Butchie believed that he was telling the truth. But how trustworthy were his sources? The more I thought about it, though, the more certain I was that the job was legit. If this were a setup, why use a bank all the way out in California? Why not pick one in Ohio? And why say the money was Nixon's? The bait could have been any big score. This job was far too complicated for a trap. The feds aren't that creative.

Knowing I wouldn't hear back from Butchie for another week, I figured the next steps were to buy a new blow car with California plates and find a place to stay while we pulled off the score. Both tasks would be easy enough. But we also needed to haul our tools and dynamite out to California. That would be a bit more complicated.

I talked with my brother and Chuck about flying out west and checking the tools in our luggage. But we didn't want to fly with the dynamite and blasting caps. The penalty for that kind of thing was a life sentence. And if the dynamite exploded while we were in the air, then we'd go down with everyone else. There was no way in hell I was going to die like that.

The other option was to drive everything out either packed up with us when we made the trip or ahead of time with one of our guys. But even though it wasn't likely that our man would be pulled over, it was possible. If that happened, the state trooper would check the glove compartment and trunk. Our job could be blown that easily.

After talking it out for a while, I finally had an idea. A friend of mine drove for United Van Lines, hauling people's crap across the country. I decided to check with him to see if any loads were heading out towards Los Angeles or Las Vegas in the coming weeks.

We got lucky. My friend was scheduled to run a shipment out to L.A. on February 26. That was perfect timing, since we had planned the job for the weekend of March 17. My friend agreed to pack my stash in with his load for three hundred dollars.

At the end of January, Chuck, my brother, and I flew out to Palm Springs. We were determined to buy our blow car and find a place to stay. Before we left, my brother called an old friend who lived in the area—a thief from Canton who had segued into gun running in the 1950s. He picked us up at the airport. Then we borrowed our friend's car and drove to Los Angeles. After searching the want ads, we found a gold 1962 Oldsmobile that sounded perfect.

Chuck and I went to look at the car. We liked what we saw. The car was in good condition, and we thought the gold paint job was a good omen for the job. We bought the car under a bogus name and took it in to have the brakes checked, the oil changed, and the tires replaced. We had to have a car in top working order in case we needed to make a quick getaway.

Next, Chuck bought a toggle switch. He mounted it under the dashboard, wiring it into the tail and stoplight circuits so that the driver could control the lights. That way, the driver could switch off everything if he needed to stop during a score. The last thing you wanted was your taillights announcing your location.

The final alteration was a false bottom in the trunk. That would serve as a perfect hiding place for our tools and the loot. The Oldsmobile had a big trunk with a deep tire well that had plenty of room. We built the false bottom with a plywood lid to cover the tire well. Next, we fit a piece of rug over the wood. We then laid the spare tire, car jack, and tire wrench on the rug to keep everything in place.

With the car ready to go, our next job was finding a place to stay.

I was thinking about the condos by the bank, but my brother and Chuck were still against the idea. They claimed the condos were too close to our target. I stood my ground.

"Who the hell is going to know we're there? The feds won't have any idea where to start looking." Without a rat to tell them anything, there was no way the FBI would find us. I fought more viciously. In the end, I won.

With that settled, I called my nephew, Harry "Ace" Barber. I told him about the score, leaving out Tricky Dick's money. See, I trusted Ace, but his inexperience had caused him to talk a little too much back in the 1960s. *This* score was way too big to risk Ace having that kind of information.

I asked if his brother, Ronnie, could rent the condo for us. Ronnie was a Vietnam veteran with a clean record. Anyone would rent to him without a second thought. He was more than happy to help set up our base.

Ronnie leased a condo from March 8 to June 7 for a thousand dollars. We finally had our hideout. I gave Ace two hundred dollars to stock up some food so we wouldn't have to worry about being seen by our neighbors. On February 26, I met the United Van Lines trucker outside of Los Angeles. I picked up our tools and dynamite. Everything was coming together.

After all that, we flew back to Ohio. I met up with Butchie to get Hoffa's cut straightened out. This haul was going to be serious money, and I wanted to settle everything before we returned to California.

Butchie said Hoffa had agreed to the 5 percent. That made me feel good, but not nearly as good as when he reached into his pocket and handed me a slip of paper.

"Here are the box numbers," Butchie said. "But it gets better. Most of the cash is in five-hundred- and one-thousand-dollar bills. Can you believe that?"

The news chilled me. I asked how Hoffa could possibly know that. The only people who could know what the loot looked like were the President and whoever had hidden the money for him. I couldn't help but think that there was more to this whole thing than Butchie or I knew.

Besides that, I knew from all my experience beating bank vaults that bills that large were rare. I had handled thousand-dollar bills from the barbotte games, exchanging them for twenties so the gamblers would bet more. I couldn't believe that now we might be stealing twenty-five or thirty thousand bills like that. The idea seemed crazy. But I liked it.

There was an upside to larger bills, too. They would be easier to carry out of the bank. The sheer weight would be much less than if the haul was thirty million in C-notes. However, laundering the larger bills would be much trickier. The only place I could pull off that kind of stunt would be Las Vegas. That would be difficult and expensive but not a huge problem.

I was just getting ready to leave when Butchie dropped his second piece of news on me. He asked if I remembered his cousin, Phil Christopher, and Phil's partner, Charley Broeckels. I said that I had known both of them for several years. They were house burglars and stick-up men as well as pill poppers. Butchie asked if I would consider taking them on the score.

"Are you crazy?" I couldn't believe Butchie was even bringing this up. Before he could say anything else, I asked if he had already told them about the score.

"No way in hell," he said. "I'd never do that." He admitted that Phil needed some big cash to buy his way off of probation. "You wouldn't have to tell them it's Tricky Dick's money. Just say it's a big score."

"Phil is a cold-blooded murderer," I said. "The word is he shot that pimp Ernie Prunella in the back of his head. He took out Dr. Price when they broke into his house. And those aren't the only dead bodies at his feet." I had even heard that one guy who Phil shot and buried wasn't dead yet. He supposedly dug himself out of the ground. I was furious at Butchie. He knew how big this score was and was risking it on two loose cannons like Phil and Broeckels.

"At least they're not rats for the law," Butchie said. "Besides, I feel bad for Phil. He's a good guy. I'd like to see him make some cash for a change and buy his way off of probation."

In the end, I let Phil and Broeckels in on the score, just so long as they wouldn't find out anything about Nixon's money. It was a favor to Butchie. I figured we'd use them as mules to carry the loot back to the condo. That would be no small job. The haul could be heavy as shit.

I didn't know yet, but that decision would turn out to be a fatal mistake.

CHAPTER FIVE

Good to Go

We returned to California on March 15. We planned to blow a hole in the bank's vault on the night of March 17. We wanted to have as much time in the vault as possible to open boxes, so we decided to take the tools to the scene the night we arrived. There was a perfect spot by the church on the parkway, only a short, downhill walk to the bank. Around midnight, we would move the tools to a bush behind the bank.

Just after it got dark that evening, my brother and I unloaded the tools at the sandy turnaround. We pushed them twenty feet deep into a heavy brush. We figured that on Thursday night, we would fill the sandbags, cut a hole in the bank's roof, and move our tools into the crawl space between the roof and the top of the vault. Then everything would be in place when we were ready to beat the alarm and blow the vault on Friday.

Shortly after midnight, my brother, Chuck, and I returned to the turnaround. We couldn't believe it, but there was a camper parked there. There were two men and two women sitting outside in front of a small TV. We couldn't figure out what they were doing. More importantly, we had no idea when they were going to leave.

For the next several hours, we sat and watched. The camper didn't show any signs of moving. By the time three o'clock rolled around, we knew it was too late to retrieve the tools. We would just have to work faster the next night. As daylight broke, we finally walked back to the condo. We decided to try picking up the tools during the day. We would watch for a break in traffic.

We woke up on Thursday, March 16, with the tools on our minds. It was only eight o'clock, but I told Chuck, "You drive. My brother and I will jump out and throw the tools in the trunk of the blow car." We hated to leave the condo so early. There were always a few men outside around that time, and we definitely didn't want them seeing our faces. But we knew it might be our only chance to grab the tools before morning traffic got too heavy.

Chuck peeked out the front door. He didn't spot anyone, so we headed to the car and were on our way. As we approached the turnaround, we saw that three cars had replaced the camper on the sandy patch off the road. A small group stood looking out over the valley. They were probably catching some early morning vistas before heading off to sightsee. I was pissed off. But not wanting to draw attention, we drove by without stopping.

We knew that the people wouldn't be able to see the tools in the underbrush, but we were still anxious about leaving everything there. We continued down the parkway to the Coast Highway, heading farther south to kill time. We hoped the cars would leave the turnaround sooner rather than later.

The Pacific Coast Highway sat two hundred and fifty feet below the shopping center. From the road, you could look up and see the back top half of the stores. The embankment leading up to the stores was covered with thick brush. Just a little ways down the highway, there was a small, circular turn-in. Seeing the turn-in, my brother, Chuck, and I thought it would be a good place to hide Tricky Dick's money from Phil, Broeckels, and Ace.

Back at the turnaround, there was still one car. Not wanting to risk stopping, we decided to let the tools sit until later that night.

After dark, we left the condo and walked to where the tools were hidden. Luckily, there was no sign of a camper, cars, or anything else that had delayed us over the last twenty-four hours. But when we reached the spot where we had left the tools, there was nothing there.

"This is where we put them, right?" my brother asked. "What the fuck?"

I couldn't believe my eyes. "It sure as hell is. Do you think those campers stole them?" We had watched the people in the camper most of the night, so I doubted they were responsible. But I had no idea who else would have done it.

"Maybe the police," Chuck said.

"No way." I was certain the police were too stupid for that. "They're not out here looking in the bushes for tools."

We searched the area but couldn't find any sign of the tools. We didn't know what to do next. My brother and Chuck were still worried that the police were wise to the score. They were afraid that if we broke into the vault now, the FBI would be waiting. I thought that was ridiculous. I said we would just have to put together more tools and go after the vault the following weekend.

Months later, we found out that a man out walking his dog had found the tools. He turned them over to the police. Just as I had thought, the police had no idea what the tools were for. At the time, we had no clue how they had disappeared.

Luckily, I still had the dynamite buried along the path leading to the shopping center, so we wouldn't need more of that. We decided that my brother and Ace would fly back to Ohio and get another drilling gear-head drive made. Because of time pressure, they would have to check the driller through in their luggage on the way back. Meanwhile, I would replace the rest of our kit with tools I could find in Southern California. The task wasn't difficult. By the following Tuesday, my brother and Ace were back with another driller and more core drilling bits. After a lot of frustration, we were finally ready to go again.

With Phil and Broeckels joining our crew, our general plan had to change. On Thursday night, Chuck and Broeckels would walk the path to the shopping center. There, they would keep an eye out for pedestrians. Ace would drop off my brother, Phil, and me behind the bank with the tools. Then he would head back to the condo to monitor the police scanner. While my brother and I were on the roof drilling, Phil would stand watch with a shotgun. I knew he wanted to blow the vault with us, but there was no way I was letting him near the haul until we got Tricky Dick's money out.

All day Wednesday, we sat around eating, playing cards, and watching TV. We waited for darkness, a burglar's best friend. When night fell outside our windows, Chuck and I took a walk across the golf course and down the path to the shopping plaza. I was focused on getting into the vault. I wanted to watch the area first to make sure we hadn't missed anything.

We had the portable police scanner and a walkie-talkie. When we reached the plaza, we cut off the path and walked along the blacktop up to the hillside, about forty yards from the bank. From there, we could see the plaza's entrance, the front of the bank, and all the storefronts clear to the supermarket. It was the perfect crow's nest for a lookout.

Nothing was coming over the scanner. That felt ghostly, as though there wasn't even a police force in Laguna Niguel. I assumed it was just a low crime area—another factor working in our favor. After we beat the bank, all of that would sure as hell change. That just shows you how stupid law enforcement can be. This bank was a sitting duck—poor security, no on-site protection, and a vault filled with Nixon's cash—but no one was keeping an eye on it. It wouldn't be until *after* we broke into the place that the cops would swarm the area, sitting in their cars or behind bushes to keep watch. All that effort would come too late.

We watched cars come and go. It looked like a regular shopping day. As it got later, the traffic died down. The cleaning crew came and went. Finally, the plaza was dead. There were just a few cars over by the bar. The bank was ready to be plucked, only protected by an alarm system that wouldn't even protect a chicken coop. I was willing to bet the President didn't even know how poorly protected his money was. Oh well, I thought. That's his goddamn problem.

A police call eventually came over the scanner. Two Mexican-Americans had robbed a gas station at gunpoint. They made off with cash and cigarettes. That was the most crime we had heard of since coming to California.

We spent the rest of the night watching the area. At dawn, we finally headed back to the condo to sleep.

On Thursday, I had Chuck and Ace take the blow car, with the tools hidden in the trunk, to Ace's garage. They wiped down all of the equipment with gloves and mineral oil; we always used the mineral oil to get our fingerprints off the tools. After that, they put the cutting torch, its hoses, and the small acetylene tank with the two small tanks of air and a tarp in a large camouflage bag. The gear-head drilling motor and the concrete drill bits went in another bag. The remaining small tools, including the liquid Styrofoam we would use to silence the alarm bell, were stashed in one of the burlap bags.

I had them place two one-gallon cans of roofing tar—to seal the hole we had cut in the plywood roof—in a separate burlap bag. The twenty-pound sledge and the B&O—a railroad tool we used to punch out the locks on the safety deposit boxes—went in another burlap bag. I told them to leave the twelve-gauge shotgun out in case we needed it in a hurry. Once the tools were wiped down and stored in their proper bags, Chuck and Ace loaded them into the trunk of the car and drove back to the condo.

Thursday night finally arrived. It was warm—warmer than Youngstown, at least. Shortly after nine o'clock, Chuck and Broeckels set out towards the plaza with walkie-talkies and a police scanner. Broeckels positioned himself next to the supermarket at the far end of the plaza. From there, he could watch for anyone who might wander down behind the stores. We had to be certain the coast was clear before driving down to the bank.

I told Chuck to stand where we had been the previous night and to let us know when the drugstore closed for the evening. As soon as he saw them leaving, he would give us the green light. Then we could swing around the back of the supermarket, drive down behind the stores, and pull up at the rear of the bank to unload the tools. If we saw any problems, like a walker spotting the car or someone still working in one of the stores, we could always come back later.

As soon as the drugstore closed, Chuck gave us the call. Everything looked good. There were still a few cars by the supermarket and bar, including one with a couple of lovers inside, but that wouldn't be a problem. I told Chuck we were on our way.

Ready to go, Ace cracked the condo's door and looked out. Seeing it was all clear, he led my brother, Phil, and me out to the blow car. We drove behind the bank and dropped our tools off. As we approached the entrance to the plaza, I called Chuck to let him know that the car coming in was ours. He answered immediately, "Come on over. It's 10-4."

We turned into the shopping center and drove straight up the front, past the bar and the car with the lovers. Then we turned up around the corner of the supermarket and drove down behind the other stores. We stopped about fifteen yards from the door of the bank. Phil got out and opened the trunk, and my brother and I unloaded the tools. With everything out of the car, Ace headed back to the condo to listen to the police scanners. We didn't think anyone had seen us. We moved the tools into the heavy bushes. I gave Chuck a call to let him know that we were all set.

"Mission accomplished," I said.

"Ten-four," came the response. I called Broeckels and told him to walk down behind the stores and over to our position.

We immediately went to work filling the burlap bags with sand—forty to fifty pounds apiece—until we had twenty or so bags ready to put on the bank's roof. When the bags of sand were ready, my brother and I took a length of rope. We climbed up the conduit pipe behind the drugstore to the roof. Then we crossed over to the roof of the bank.

I lowered the rope down to Phil. I told him to tie the bag of tools on it, so I could pull them up. Then I took a wire cutter, a razor knife, black electrical tape, and the female electrical receptacle and went over to one of the air conditioner units. I was ready to open an electrical panel box to tie in the female receptacle. But then I remembered that we needed to get the extension ladder, which Phil had stolen from a neighboring church. I told my brother to send Phil for it.

Opening the electrical box, I immediately saw it was 220 volts, single phase, and I knew that each electric power line coming to the unit was carrying 110 volts of electric current. I figured I'd splice in my female receptacle and take one wire to one of the 110-volt feeder lines and the other wire to an earth ground in the electric panel. That would give us the 110 volts we needed to operate our power tools. I was about to splice in when I saw there already was a 110-volt receptacle outlet on the unit. I couldn't believe my luck.

By then, it was a little after midnight. I told my brother to get the saber saw and cut the hole in the roof. He picked a spot and checked with me.

"That looks good," I told him. "Cut right over the middle of the vault."

Using an L-bar, my brother scraped the roof gravel away. I jammed another L-bar through the tarpaper, ripping both the paper and the roof insulation away from the plywood. Then my brother cut a thirty-six inch round hole in the plywood. As he worked, I held the cutout piece so it wouldn't fall through the hole and hit the top of the concrete vault. That would set off the bank's alarm system for sure.

After the hole was cut, I lowered the extension cord lamp down to get a better view of the crawl space. We had about seven or eight feet down to the top of the vault, which was farther than I had originally estimated. By then, Phil was back with the ladder, and we lowered the rope so that he could secure it and allow us to pull it up. Sliding the ladder into the hole, we climbed down.

Now we were sitting on top of the vault.

"I wonder how thick this baby is," my brother said, tapping it.

"Probably twenty-four inches, like the others we've beaten," I told him. At that point, we finally had a chance to take a close look at the concrete. I saw that there were hundreds of small hairline cracks running every which way through it. That was great to see. Those assholes had definitely used a cheap grade of concrete when they poured the vault.

On a bank vault job, the first thing we did to prepare to blast a hole was to drill a three-eighths inch pilot hole all the way through the concrete to find out how thick the concrete is. That helps us determine how much dynamite we need. But on this vault, judging from what we could see from the top of the concrete, it wouldn't take much to crack her.

The most important thing we had to do that night was get the sandbags on top of the vault. Let me tell you, I was glad my brother and I were both as strong as gorillas. Pulling up those bags was hard work. While we worked, Chuck radioed to warn us that the cleaning crew had arrived. We waited on the roof for them to leave. Once they were gone, we finished putting the bags of sand, the tools, and the rest of our rope on top of the vault.

With everything in place, we drilled four quarter-inch holes on the outside of the circle around the cutout hole in the roof. We then bolted four small pieces of plywood to the underside. We laid the cut piece of roof plywood on top of the four six-inch pieces we bolted to the roof. Then we spread tar around the saw cut made in the plywood. That way no water could leak in. With that done, we still had to use roof gravel to fill in the area of the hole so that it was level, making up the space left from the insulation being removed. (See diagram on page 56.) When all was said and done, even a repairman that might need to go up on the roof would never be able to spot our work.

As an added precaution, I used the gravel on the roof to prop up a small piece of mirror. That way, we could drive by and look down at the bank's roof to see if anyone had disturbed our work. I also lined up several pieces of larger gravel in a straight line right over the hole. If anything was disturbed, we would know.

By then it was four in the morning. Most of the hard preparation work was done. With dawn approaching, we all headed back to the condo. We were exhilarated, but we knew that the real test would come the following night. Tomorrow we would blow the vault and steal millions of Tricky Dick's dirty dollars.

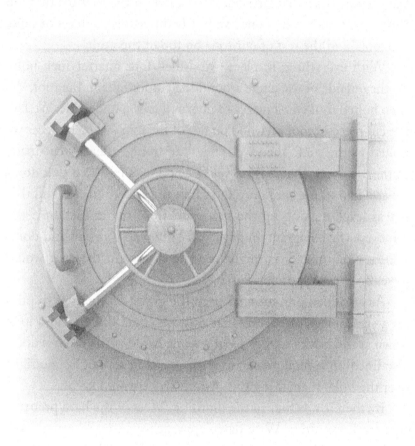

CHAPTER SIX

Where No Thief Has Gone Before

On Friday, we rested and took turns listening to the police scanner. Luckily, there was no word on a bank burglary in Laguna Niguel. We figured we were in the clear. Just in case, though, I drove over to the parkway to see if the mirror had been disturbed. I could see the sun's reflection. Everything looked good.

I pulled into the plaza and sat in the parking lot for a few minutes. Customers flowed in and out of the bank as usual. The bank was doing business, its employees and customers unaware that burglars' tools were sitting on top of their vault. I felt bad for them. They had no idea what was going to happen that night. It just goes to show you, what you don't know *can* hurt you.

At nine o'clock, I told Chuck to take a walkie-talkie, a scanner, and the binoculars, and head to his lookout position. By half past ten, the rest of us started walking across the golf course to the bank. Ace stayed behind to keep an ear on the police scanners.

As we walked, my mind was in overdrive. I couldn't stop wondering about that thirty million. I knew we couldn't mess this up. This was the score of a lifetime. I didn't want to blow the score, and I really wanted the satisfaction of stealing Tricky Dick's dirty money.

We stopped on the way to retrieve the dynamite and blasting caps from where I had buried them. My brother carried the blasting caps and I carried the dynamite. The worst thing you can do is carry those two things together. I imagined all of us, exploded, on the pavement.

As we approached the plaza, I called Chuck. He said everything looked good, so we headed down to the bank. Along the way, we heard a door slam. We scrambled for cover and squatted in the bushes, listening. We didn't see any cars or lights. Eventually, we took a chance and kept walking.

Behind the bank, we hid in the bushes and waited for the drugstore to close. I'm a pretty jolly guy, but when I'm after a bank vault, all bets are off. I become a different person. I'm serious and focused only on the money. As we waited, I kept rehearsing the plan in my head. The first thing my brother and I would do in the vault would be to knock out the locks on Nixon's boxes. Then we would sack up the money and get the hell out of there. We could hide the stash at the turnaround on the Coast Highway. I just didn't know how we would get past Phil, Broeckels, and Ace. I didn't want those small-time crooks to see Tricky Dick's cash.

I was also worried that the thirty million would be in small notes. Butchie had assured me the money would be in five-hundred- and one-thousand-dollars bills. But what if he was wrong? How the hell would my brother and I hide all that cash? I played a lot of different options through my head, and some were downright awful—but this haul was *that* important to me. In the end, I didn't act on anything I thought. Instead, I decided to wait and see what happened.

Chuck called to say the drugstore had closed. I went up to the bank roof to make sure none of our work had been discovered. Everything looked just like we had left it. I paused on top of the roof to savor the moment, letting the night collect on my face. I lived for moments like these.

Then I had to get back to work. I crept to the edge of the roof and told my brother to come up. We were good to go.

My brother and I removed the gravel from the top of the hole, uncovering the tarred saw cut around the circle in the plywood. I pried up the cutout piece of wood with my penknife. I flipped it over, leaving the hole open. The tar was sticky, which was a problem. Our ladder, the sandbags, and our other tools were down below on the vault. If we slid over the edge of the hole, we would have tar all over our chests. That was the last thing we wanted. So I gave Phil a call on the walkie-talkie and told him to look in the dumpsters behind the stores for large pieces of cardboard or garbage bags. He found some cardboard, and we laid it around the edges of the hole. You have to think creatively on a job like this.

With the buffer in place, I slid cleanly over the edge. My brother held onto one of my hands to keep me from dropping. From this precarious position, I eased myself down onto the pile of sandbags, and then I grabbed the ladder and positioned it for my brother. With both of us in position, I climbed back up the ladder with the extension cord. Then I plugged it into the rooftop air conditioning unit.

Now we had light and power to run our tools.

We knew the cleaning crew would arrive soon. I couldn't go down into the bank to cut the alarm before they left, so we just waited on the roof. Once it was safe, I slid my pocketknife down between the ceiling tile and its steel frame, raising the edge of the tile until I could lift it out of place. Then I lowered myself down to the bank's floor.

Once I had safely landed, I turned on my penlight and moved down the hallway. I found the telephone junction box and removed the two red caps. Forty years have passed since that night, so I'm not sure what tactic I used. I might have strung a piece of copper wire between one brass terminal post and the other; or I might have just skinned the plastic covering on the phone wires and twisted them together to make a good connection. Either way, I beat the alarm.

Telephones operate on two phone wires. So after I beat the circuit alarm, I disconnected one phone wire from each of the five sets of brass terminals. That way, if the bank also had a dialer alarm, it wouldn't be able to dial out to the police. I, then, replaced the red caps on the alarm terminals and cut the two alarm wires heading back to the alarm control panel in the vault. Now the vault was unprotected. All that was left to do was put the liquid Styrofoam into the alarm bell.

I peered up at my brother through the hole. "The alarms are history."

"Hell, yes," he said. "Let's get this baby."

The fridge was right there, so I took out two bottles of Coke. I handed both up to my brother. Then he pulled me back up on top of the vault, and we headed to silence the alarm bell mounted on the back wall of the bank.

My brother stretched the extension cord across to the edge of the roof. Then he plugged in the electric drill. Phil and Broeckels helped me position the ladder against the side of the building. Because the ladder was too short to reach from the blacktop to the top of the roof, I eased myself over the edge as my brother tethered me with the rope. He lowered me down until my feet were resting on the top rung of the ladder.

Next, I crept down a few rungs until I was just below the bottom of the bell. My brother lowered the drill down to me on the end of the extension cord. Putting the drill in reverse, I backed out the only bolt that didn't have a tamper switch. The other three were rigged to set off the alarm if you loosened them.

After I had the bolt backed out, I filled the resulting hole with liquid Styrofoam. The substance hardened and froze the bell's clapper. That would stop the bell from ringing. Next, I reversed the drill and put the bolt back in the bell's housing. After this was all in place, I made my way up to the roof and prepared to start drilling the holes in the concrete.

After my brother lowered himself back down into the crawl space, he scratched five Xs where we would drill the five blasting holes in the concrete. (See diagram on page 56.)

We then put a 3/8 inch carbon tipped drilling bit in the drill chuck on the gear-head motor my brother had built, and my brother went to drilling. The drilling bit cut down through the concrete as if it was drilling a hole in frozen butter. As soon as the drill chuck touched the concrete, the hole was eleven inches deep. We then put a 12 inch extension in the drill chuck and kept on drilling until the drill bit was all the way through the concrete. This concrete was the softest concrete of any vault we had ever blasted a hole into.

I slid my measuring tape down into the hole until it reached the bottom. The hole was eighteen inches deep. That was six inches shorter than the concrete in other vaults we had blasted.

After evaluating all of the thousands of small hairline cracks running in all directions in the concrete, we figured we should reduce the amount of dynamite in each hole. The last thing we wanted was to destroy the entire vault and blow the score.

We put a twelve inch long, one inch Tilden core-drilling bit in the drill chuck and went to drilling. The drill bit was moving so fast into the concrete that I told my brother to make each hole eleven inches deep instead of nine inches. With the poor grade of concrete, the deeper holes would crack the vault like a nut.

The holes each took less than three minutes to drill.

"Don't jump too hard on the vault," my brother said. "With this shitty concrete, we could fall through into the vault." We both laughed.

/ 56 / Inside the Vault

United California Bank
500 Safety deposit boxes inside its vault.

One mile from the bank. Man in condominium is monitoring radio transmission from state police, local police and the Orange County Sheriff's Office. He has walkie-talkie comunication with the lookout man in the bushes outside of the bank and with the burglars inside the bank.

Getting Inside The Vault

Air Conditioner

Electic Extension Cord

Walkie-Talkie

Man on ladder injecting liquid Styrofoam into the outside alarm bell. Foam borders inside the bell's housing and the bell's clapper is frozen. The bell can't ring.

Lowering tools through the hole in the bank's roof, down to the top of the vault.

Phone line junction box. Man shown bypassing the bank's silent alarm going to the police.

Five 1" holes, drilled 11" deep into the 18" of reinforced concrete on top of the vault. Each hole has approximately 2 ounces of 60% nitroglycerin dynamite and an electric blasting cap in it.

Plywood Roof
1 inch thick

Wall of sand bags used as protection during detonation

Lookout man in the bushes with a walkie-talkie.

Vault Door

The only problem was when the drill bit hit a rebar. But we just moved over an inch or so and started drilling again. The second time went as smooth as silk.

With all the holes drilled, it was time to load the explosives. The dynamite we were using was made with 60 percent nitroglycerin and some sawdust. The sawdust absorbs the liquid nitroglycerin so the dynamite becomes gooey. Then the substance can be shaped into any form.

My brother, an expert in explosives, took an egg-shaped chunk of dynamite. He squeezed it around an electric blasting cap, sculpting it like a miniature hot dog and fitting it down the 1-inch wide by 11-inch deep hole. Once each dynamite piece was ready, I lowered it into one of the holes. Soon all five were loaded. Then we wired the five blasting caps into a series. We left the two remaining blasting cap wire ends so we could touch them to an electric source. That was the last step in setting off an explosive. (See diagram, page 59.)

After the dynamite was set in each hole, we filled each cavity with a mixture of sand and water. Years of experience had taught us that this procedure would direct the force of the blast downward. That would send most of the crushed concrete into the vault. Most of the sound from the explosion would disappear into the vault, too, which was a nice bonus.

Next, we placed our folded tarp over the five holes so that no pieces of blasted concrete could fly out. Crisscrossing the bags of sand over the tarp to hold it down, we were ready to set off the dynamite. By then, it was two in the morning. I was anxious to get into the vault and find Nixon's dirty money.

"We'll have a hole in this baby in a few minutes," my brother assured me.

I called Chuck on the walkie-talkie, told him we were ready to make some noise and asked him to keep watch for anyone who might hear. Phil called to say it looked good in back. Everything was ready.

My brother and I lay flat on the concrete behind a pile of sandbags. Then I took the two wires leading from the blasting caps and placed one end on one side of the extension cord's receptacle. Then, Chuck gave us an all clear, so I put the end of the other blasting cap wire in the other side of the receptacle. There was a muffled, booming sound, and a jarring vibration rattled through our bodies. The sandbags covering the blast area jumped about eight inches and then fell down into the new hole in the vault.

"Christ," said my brother. "That was fucking perfect."

"No shit," I said. "No one could have heard that."

Just as we had expected, the concrete was weak. Most of the sound from the explosion went into the vault. Moving the sandbags, we found that the blast was one of our best. The procedure was both quiet and effective.

Seconds later, Chuck called on the radio. "Was that it?"

"No shit," I said. "What did it sound like out there?"

"I could barely hear anything. Did it even make a hole?"

I laughed and told him it had. "Now stop calling. We have work to do."

We removed the tarp. Holding the light over the hole, I could see straight through the crisscrossed rebars to the floor of the vault. We were in. Adrenaline rushed through me.

Now all we had to do was suck the nitroglycerin fumes out of the vault. If we didn't, we'd have headaches for days. Then we had to cut the rebars off so we could lower a ladder through the hole and down to the vault floor.

We usually used a small electric exhaust suction blower to remove the fumes, but I had forgotten that the roof was eight feet up from the floor of the vault. That meant that our exhaust hose would be too short. We had to remove two of the ceiling tiles just off of the edge of the vault, which created a draft like that of a house chimney. I held the exhaust hose up to the hole in the roof, and my brother turned on the blower. In ten minutes, the fumes were gone.

DIAGRAM OF DRILLING HOLES INTO A BANK'S CONCRETE VAULT; AND WIRING EXPLOSIVES WITH ELECTRIC DETONATOR BLASTING CAPS FOR BLASTING A HOLE INTO THE VAULT.

First you have to beat the Bank's alarm system. Then you get on top of the Bank's concrete vault. Then by using a 3/8" concrete drilling bit, you drill a hole all the way through the concrete. This is done to determine how thick the concrete is, which is usually 18" to 24".

Lets say it is 24" thick. That means that you will drill 5 one inch holes (as shown in the diagram) using a concrete drill bit, each hole 12" deep, which is half of the 24" of concrete. That will center the blast in the middle of the concrete. Concrete is brittle, meaning it will easily crack up into small pieces.

After the 5 holes are drilled, you load each hole with 2 ounces of 60% nitroglycerine dynamite (even 40% will do) or about one and a half ounces of C-4 explosives with one electric detonator blasting cap in each of the 5 holes. Each detonator blasting cap has 2 small copper wires leading out of it. Each wire is a different color. The diagram shows a red wire and a black wire. The colors don't matter.

You then wire the blasting caps in a series from one hole to the other (as shown in the diagram) winding up with 2 blasting wire ends to touch to a battery to set off the blasting cap, which in return sets of the explosives in the hole. Almost any battery will work. You can even use the 110 volt receptacle in the Bank. The electric power source, sends an electric charge to the blasting cap. There is a small "BOOM" and a hole is blasted through the concrete. Cut some re-bars left in the hole, then

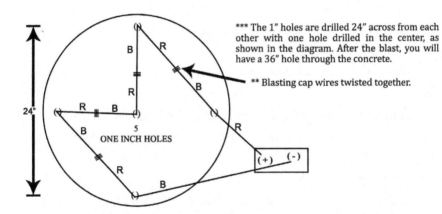

*** The 1" holes are drilled 24" across from each other with one hole drilled in the center, as shown in the diagram. After the blast, you will have a 36" hole through the concrete.

** Blasting cap wires twisted together.

However, before setting off the blasting caps, you must stack 15 or 20, 40 to 50 pound bags of dirt over the 5 holes and put a tarp over the bags. The dirt forces the blast downward, taking most of the concrete with it into the Bank's vault. It also stops small pieces of concrete from flying around. WARNING. If you are thinking about blasting a hole into a Bank vault, using this method or even thinking about using explosives for any reason, you should first familiarize yourself with explosives. You make one screw up—mistake, your dead or missing some of your body parts.

Once the rebars were cut and the ladder lowered, I sent down the extension cord light. With everything in place, I climbed down the ladder. Now I was finally inside the vault. My brother was right behind. I hit the vault lights. An entire wall was covered with hundreds of stainless steel safety deposit box doors and brass keyhole locks. The whole room shined.

Bingo.

I wanted to linger and take in the amazing sight. But unless I wanted to die in here, I needed to make sure all of the alarm systems were cut. I couldn't find a telephone dialer alarm control panel, so I knew the vault had only been protected by a circuit alarm. I went up the ladder and back down into the bank. There, I replaced the phone line wires I had disconnected in the telephone junction box. Now if anyone came into the bank and wanted to use the phone, they wouldn't have any idea that the alarm system had been tampered with.

With all of the alarms silenced, it was time to start opening boxes.

All safety deposit boxes have numbers engraved in the door. We quickly found the numbers Butchie had given us. To this day, I still remember those numbers. I can picture those shiny boxes so clearly in my mind. We had come so far. I savored the moment.

Tricky Dick's boxes were huge. They had been placed along the lower row of the wall. I held the B&O tool against the first brass lock keyhole, and my brother hit the back of the B&O with the sledge. The B&O got its name from the Baltimore and Ohio Railroad. It was originally a tool designed for driving railroad spikes into place. Over the years, we had found it perfect for knocking locks out of safety deposit boxes. One smack from the sledge and the brass lock was driven back into the metal box. With the B&O punch still on the lock cylinder hole, I gave it a tug to the right. The door swung open.

I pulled the box out of its steel frame—it weighed about thirty pounds—and set it on a stepping stool. Then I lifted the long metal lid covering the box opening. The box was packed with brown paper packages, stacked front to back. There were ten in all. We knew they were full of dirty money.

My brother pulled out one of the packs. There were no marks on the paper. Tearing the wrapper off, we saw that the money was in the form of new hundred-dollar bills. Each package contained ten separate packs of C-notes. There was a ten-thousand-dollar money wrapper around each pack.

The wrapper had the Federal Reserve Bank seal.

I looked through the bills. The serial numbers ran in sequence. That meant the pack was worth one hundred thousand dollars. We were excited. We ripped the other nine packages open. Each one contained hundred-dollar bills. From what we could tell, all of the bills had the Federal Reserve Seal of Dallas, Texas printed on them. They were obviously the work of John Connally. In the back of the box, there were also twenty or so twenty-dollar gold coins in a Canadian Royal Crown bottle bag. We thought that was classy.

We punched out the lock on Nixon's next box. Inside were two Kroger Store shopping bags. The bags were folded over and taped shut. There were also books of coins and gold railroad watches in clear plastic cases.

We knew the bags had to hold money. My brother tore one open. Sure enough, it was filled with envelopes of thousand-dollar bills. The other Kroger bag held envelopes stuffed with five-hundred-dollar bills.

I knew the Federal Reserve Bank had stopped issuing five-hundred-, one-thousand-, five-thousand-, and ten-thousand-dollar bills at that point. In 1969, the Reserve even began withdrawing those large bills from circulation. I worried that it would be tricky to get the money laundered, but I figured we would deal with that in Vegas.

At the writing of this book in 2012, the World Almanac shows there are still 142,360 five-hundred-dollar bills and 165,644 one-thousand-dollar bills in circulation. I wonder where those bills are hiding. They must be stashed away in safety deposit boxes somewhere—just like the boxes we busted into.

We filled burlap sacks with all the cash and threw the gold coins and railroad watches into another bag.

"I think we hit the mother lode," I told my brother. I could barely contain my excitement.

"And daddy's lode, too," he said, laughing.

We didn't have time to count the money, but we could tell it couldn't add up to the thirty million Butchie had promised. Nonetheless it was a huge haul. We were pleased. When we finally sat down and went through everything, we discovered that we had stolen twelve million dollars from Tricky Dick.

The loot only weighed about forty pounds. That was lucky. I knew my brother and I would have to figure out how to slip it past Phil and Broeckels. We snuck back onto the bank roof and crept over the store roofs. Phil and Broeckels, who were still positioned behind the bank, couldn't see anything.

Just before we reached the supermarket, we climbed down an electric conduit at the back of the building and jumped to the blacktop. Leaving my brother to stand guard, I took the bag down the hill to the Coast Highway. I stashed it in the brush by the turnaround. I felt chills hiding so much money in public.

By the time we got back to the vault, we were exhausted. We opened several more boxes but didn't find anything that excited us. Since dawn was creeping closer, we took the few valuables from the other boxes and headed out of the vault. Then we sealed the hole in the roof and replaced our mirror. At that point, we were safe to climb back down to the blacktop. I called Chuck and told him to meet us at the path by the supermarket. We didn't have too much loot to carry that first night. But my brother and I had what we had come for: Nixon's money.

Thirty years after the robbery, a reporter for the *Orange County Register* wrote a story about our bank burglary. He claimed we never got the President's money because we had hit the wrong bank.

I bet Tricky Dick wished we had hit the wrong bank.

We made it back to the condo just fifteen minutes before daybreak. Once we were settled in, my brother and I told the others we were taking Ronnie's car to cruise by the bank and see if anyone was around. What we really planned to do was pick up our hidden loot at the turnaround. The last thing we wanted was for that money to disappear like our first set of tools. I felt panic just considering the possibility.

The plaza looked dead, so we went down the Coast Highway to the turnaround. It was too early for much traffic, so it was easy to pull into the bushes and load the bag of cash into the trunk. We took off before anyone saw us. More than anything, I remember the moments after we had the cash in the car—shaking my brother's hand and telling him that we had done it. We had pulled off the burglary of a lifetime. I never felt happier.

Back at the condo, we ate, rested, and listened to the scanners. We drove by the plaza a couple more times, but the lot was quiet. The mirror was shining on the roof. Nothing looked wrong.

Looking out over the golf course from the condo, I wondered about the millions of dollars we had stolen. I thought about how Tricky Dick and his cronies had stolen it first. I wondered who were the bigger crooks. If we got caught stealing the money, we'd be locked away for years. But what would happen to the President and other sleazy politicians for doing the same thing? As I figured, what we had done was justified thievery. This was justice between thieves.

And we were just getting started.

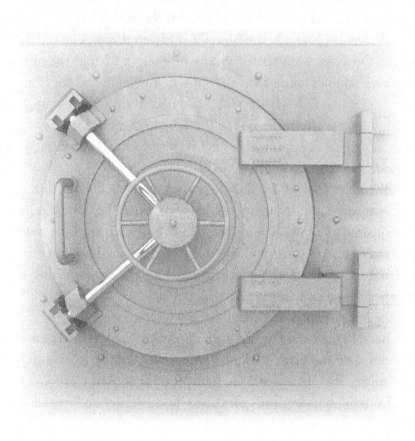

CHAPTER SEVEN

A Weekend in the Vault

The following night, we were all rested, excited, and ready to attack more of the safety deposit boxes. We had to wait until the drugstore closed, though, since the back of the vault touched that building.

At ten o'clock, we all headed to the plaza. Chuck took up his lookout position while the rest of us hid in the bushes behind the bank. We waited for word from Chuck that the drugstore had closed. Ace stayed in the condo to listen to the police scanners.

While we were waiting, I explained the plan to the others. I said that I would go up first to make sure everything looked okay. When I gave the word, my brother would come up to help unseal the hole in the roof. Then we would let Broeckels up to help with the vault.

After Chuck radioed that the drugstore had closed, I climbed up the conduit to the roof. The mirror was just as I had left it, as were the small pieces of gravel we had set up. I called for my brother and Broeckels to join me.

"Stay with the shotgun and guard the area," I told Phil. "And please don't kill anyone, okay?" I knew he wanted to come along. I liked Phil, and keeping watch was just about the only thing I trusted Phil to do. There's always the risk of people creeping around to look in dumpsters. If anyone heard noises from inside, that could blow the score. I needed someone down there who I could trust to keep watch.

After we unsealed the hole, I laid a plastic garbage bag over the sticky tar around the opening. Then my brother held my hands and lowered me down to the crawl space. There, I set up the ladder for my brother and Broeckels. But there was a problem. Broeckels' big gut made it hard for him to squeeze through the hole. At first it looked like he might get stuck. I could imagine the headlines: "Bank Burglary Foiled by Beer Gut." Luckily, though, Broeckels finally made it through.

"This sure as hell beats knocking off houses," Broeckels said.

I told him that our crew didn't like robbing from the poor. In the vault, though, we didn't know whom we were taking from. We just grabbed everything. At least we weren't in someone's house, though, creeping around in their private space.

We were still working on the big boxes along the bottom of the vault. I told Broeckels to search for valuables while my brother and I continued punching out locks. We destroyed about thirty in a row before pausing to look through the contents. On a vault job, we only take what's easy to carry and sell. We put all the jewelry in one bag, gold coins and books of coins in another, cash in a third bag, and any stocks and bonds in a fourth. Anything that didn't look valuable or would be too hard to sell was just thrown into the mess on the floor.

You would not believe some of the things we've found in safety deposit boxes. Over the years, we've recovered everything from drugs to rare sculptures.

After going through the first thirty boxes, we punched out another thirty and kept sorting. We were finding a lot of the usual stuff—cash, bonds, and jewelry—but this wasn't as big of a haul as some of our other jobs. I have always had the best luck in Florida.

Let me tell you, if you want a real score, hit a bank in Florida. The people there seem wealthier than in any other state.

We were moving along nicely, but then Chuck called with bad news. He said a car had pulled up right in front of the bank.

Broeckels panicked. "Let's get out of here." He moved for the ladder before I could stop him.

"What the hell is the matter with you?" I said. "No one knows we're in here." I called Chuck to ask if it was a police car. He said no and described what he saw. Two young guys got out of the car. One unlocked the door. The other was pulling something out of the trunk.

"It looks like a waxer," Chuck said.

I was relieved. It was just the cleaning crew making an unscheduled visit to wax and polish the floor. Although Broeckels still wanted to get out, I knew our best bet was to stay quiet and wait.

"Let's go up on the roof," Broeckels said.

I told him to be quiet. "They don't know anyone's in here. And they sure as hell can't see through the vault door." I told everyone to sit tight.

You can hear more than you would think through a vault door. We listened to the muffled sounds of the cleaning crew. They sounded like they were using buffers, but we weren't sure.

While we waited, I started thinking about the vault light switch. I wondered if there was a light outside the door that indicated when the vault lights were on. If there was an indicator light, hopefully they would just think an employee had left the lights on by accident. I sure as hell didn't want to turn the lights off now and have them notice the indicator change.

A few minutes later, Chuck radioed to say that another car was pulling into the plaza. It was a false alarm, but the call made me realize how loud our walkie-talkies were. I plugged in my earpiece so that if Chuck or Phil called, their voices wouldn't blare out for the whole world—and the cleaning crew—to hear. Chuck asked if

I wanted him to sneak around to the front and check to see what the crew was doing. I told him that wasn't worth the risk. They were probably polishing the floor. Chances were they wouldn't be in the bank much longer.

While we were trying to be as quiet as possible, Broeckels let out two hideously loud coughs.

"What the hell are you doing?" I asked.

"I couldn't help it," he said. He sounded like he was lying.

Covering his mouth with his jersey, he let out another booming cough. I sent him to the back of the vault and told him to shut up. I couldn't believe his behavior. I decided that if the cleaning crew heard someone in the vault, we'd have to leave his ass down there while we got the hell out. I tried to control my rage and told him to take a drink of water.

"It's the cigarettes," he said. "Do you think they heard me?"

"I doubt it. They're still working." I was just about to send him up the ladder in case he coughed again, but then he assured me he would be okay. The fit had passed.

After twenty minutes, I decided to climb to the top of the vault to see if I could get a better idea of what was going on. From my new height, I could hear what sounded like a floor buffer. I wondered how long they would stay. I thought about how you really never know what you'll encounter on a score. We were losing valuable time, but we had no control over the situation. All we could do was sit tight and shut up.

Once, on a night deposit safe score in Florida, we watched the bank for three straight weekends. The cleaning crew came on Saturday nights. On Sunday nights, the place was empty. This was a very busy shopping area. That meant we would get Friday, Saturday, and Sunday's night drop deposits from all the stores in the area. (See page 154 showing our jig we used to drill open Round Door Safes.)

On Sunday night, we went in. After jumping off the alarm going to the night deposit safe, we drilled the safe open. Because night deposit bags have metal locks and a lot of deposits have rolls of coins, the bags were too heavy to carry out of the bank. We always used a razor knife to cut the bags open. We would throw out the bundles of checks and rolls of coins and just bag up the cash.

We had almost all the bags cut open. There was a huge pile of money sitting on the floor when our walkie man called and said a van was pulling up. It sounded like the cleaning crew. Two guys got out of the van and headed to the door. As they came in, we could hear them talking. One of the guys said, "Let's go get a coffee first." The walkie man said they came back out and ran to their van.

"Let's get out of here," I said. "They noticed something."

My brother stuffed some bills in a burlap bag. But as we were making a quick exit out through the hole in the roof, the bag caught on the metal we had cut through and tore open. Bills rained back down into the bank. We still got away with about forty-two thousand dollars. More importantly, we were free to go after the next score. I've been through so much on scores and know more than anyone how much trouble can be out there.

While I was waiting on top of the vault in Laguna Niguel, I thought about what else we could take out. I decided that once the cleaning crew left, I would open the two safes in the back of the vault and grab the bank's operating money. It wouldn't be much, but it would be cash.

Finally, we heard the crew wrapping up. Chuck eventually radioed to say that they had left. I went down in the vault and opened the square door safes, removing the bank's operating reserve cash. I checked the bills for a tear gas cartridge—the kind that bank tellers hide in stacks and hand out to bank robbers—but there wasn't one. I put that cash in a separate bag and tied it shut. I knew that stash would contain bait bills with recorded serial numbers.

On the other side of the vault, my brother was telling Broeckels that he swung the sledge like a girl. I knew Broeckels wasn't in good enough shape to punch out the locks, so I told him to keep sorting through the boxes. Broeckels was turning out to be completely useless.

My brother and I kept moving. We punched out locks and then went through their contents with Broeckels. It was like a treasure hunt. I loved sifting through all those items for anything that might be valuable.

That night, we punched out all of the large- and medium-sized safety deposit boxes. By the time we left, the vault floor was litered with personal papers, legal documents, loose rolls of coins, and anything else not worth taking. (To see pictures of inside the vault, turn to pages 162-165.)

By four in the morning, we knew it was time to start wrapping up. We had to get out of the vault before daylight. We had about a hundred pounds of loot in burlap bags, so we moved them to the top of the vault and onto the roof of the bank. We lowered everything by rope down to the blacktop. Then my brother and I sealed the hole in the roof. I placed the mirror facing the parkway and lined up the gravel in its usual pattern. Once we were on the ground, I called Chuck to tell him we were done. Chuck radioed 10-4 and met us by the supermarket.

Since Phil was strong and hadn't done anything but sit around with the shotgun, he had the job of carrying the heavy bag of gold. My brother, Broeckels, and I also grabbed bags. We took off across the blacktop to meet up with Chuck. Together, we all walked back to the condo, stopping for breathers along the way. I don't care how strong you are—a hundred pounds of loot is heavy.

We finally made it back to the condo. We laid the bags of loot on the floor in the living room and started sorting. We weren't sure how thick the walls were, so we stayed as quiet as possible.

"That's a lot of stuff," Phil said. He turned to Broeckels. "We should go after bank vaults instead of houses. This is where the money is."

All I could think was that those idiot pill poppers wouldn't have any idea how to take on an alarm system, let alone blow a hole in a bank vault. What my brother, Chuck, and I did was skilled work, and I was proud of it. Phil and Broeckels were nothing more than home invaders. They would kill a man in his own home if he got in their way.

My brother dumped the bag of cash out on the floor. I told him not to mix the safety deposit box money with the operating cash in the other bag. Before we started counting, I told everyone we should eat. After all, we still had more boxes to punch. Counting the cash could wait until we had everything together.

"This is a lot of money," Broeckels said. "Why don't we count our blessings and forget about the rest? We should get out of the area before anyone finds out what we've done."

I didn't say anything, but my brother jumped down his throat. "Are you nuts? Didn't you see all those boxes left in there? Don't be a moron. Imagine what we could be leaving behind." Broeckels and Phil didn't say a word. That's when I knew it had been a mistake bringing those guys. They just weren't up for such a big job.

After we ate, Chuck said he would stay awake and listen to the scanners. I woke up shortly after noon. Chuck said a few calls had come over the scanners. Thankfully, there was no word on the bank.

"The only way they would know that something happened is if someone fell through that hole on the roof," I said. I sent Chuck to get some rest and took over listening to the scanner. Before he left, he suggested that I let Broeckels be the lookout man so he could help out in the vault.

"There's no way I trust Broeckels or Phil on the walkie-talkie," I said, and Chuck understood. He headed to bed with red, exhausted eyes.

While I was listening to the scanner, I started planning how we would get the loot from the condo to Ace's garage. We definitely needed to wait until after dark. We couldn't chance anyone seeing us carrying anything out of the condo ... especially not a bunch of giant, burlap bags.

I wondered if we could use our suitcases to transport everything, because we would need a lot of space for all the loot. I woke up Ace and told him to go buy six or seven Samsonite suitcases. "Get the kind with the hard plastic exteriors, sturdy latches, and strong carrying handles, okay?" We could distribute the heavy loot among the many suitcases.

When my brother woke up, I told him that I was thinking about jamming the time clocks on the vault door when we finished the job, so that the door wouldn't open on Monday morning. That would give us a few hours to clean the condo and flee the area before the burglary was discovered. Even better, a failure in the time clocks would probably be written off as a technical malfunction. No one would suspect a crime until it was too late.

"Great idea," my brother said.

With that settled, my brother put on a baseball cap and sunglasses. He took a walk on the parkway to see how things looked around the bank. In thirty minutes, he returned, saying everything looked good. When I asked how he felt, he said he didn't like Broeckels and wished we hadn't brought him. I couldn't have agreed more.

"We'll be out of here tomorrow," I promised.

While Ace was out buying the suitcases, my brother and I put on rubber gloves and counted the cash from the safety deposit boxes. We got around four hundred and twenty thousand dollars, though I don't remember the exact amount. We collected the bills in ten-thousand-dollar stacks and put them in a plastic garbage bag. The bank's cash was mostly small bills. We kept that in another garbage bag.

After counting the money, we dumped a bag of gold on the kitchen table and stacked all the coins. We put all the American gold coins in separate stacks and all the coins individually encased in plastic in a garbage bag. We put all the foreign gold coins—everything from Mexican pesos to British Sovereigns—in yet another plastic bag.

Next, we dumped out another bag of mixed coins. The silver coins, nickels, and pennies were already individually encased in clear plastic, so we put them in their own garbage bag.

While we were sorting the coins, Phil and Broeckels woke up and came into the kitchen. "Is that all gold?" Phil asked. He was stunned. "How much do you think we can get for it?"

"A lot," I said. I had to admit that the gold looked pretty good all stacked on the counter. I stopped to admire it, too.

When we had started counting, I had told everyone to wear gloves at all times. But as I was going through the coins, I saw Phil and Broeckels hunched up in the living room. They were looking through the jewelry with naked fingers.

"What are you guys doing?" I yelled. "Do you want to leave your fingerprints on everything?"

"I don't know," Broeckels said, mumbling like an idiot.

I asked if they had touched the bonds.

"A few," Phil admitted.

I was furious. I explained that the FBI could lift fingerprints left on paper.

"I didn't know that," Phil whined. He pointed out the bonds they had touched. There were just a few, lying outside the bag. I told them to put the jewelry in the bathtub with dishwashing detergent. I soaked the bonds in water, then put them in a garbage bag and dumped them. A year later, we found out that some land surveyors found the bag and turned it into the police. The FBI claimed the contents were worth between one and two million dollars. I think the FBI was dead wrong on that figure. The last time I saw the bonds, they looked like paste in the bottom of the garbage bag.

Next, we put the loot in the new suitcases, loaded them into the blow car, and drove them to Ace's house.

Now we could feel some relief. Two nights down, and one to go.

We were finally ready to get the rest of the goodies from the remaining safety deposit boxes. Chuck, my brother, and I still had Tricky Dick's money in the trunk of Ronnie's car. We assumed it would be safe there.

We left just after ten o'clock on Sunday night. Ace stayed to monitor the scanners, and Chuck headed to his lookout position. Everything at the bank looked just as we'd left it. That was a relief.

"Why not let Broeckels stand watch tonight?" Phil asked as we waited for the drugstore to close. Phil would have been more helpful in the vault, but I decided against the idea. I told him we needed someone on the shotgun who was strong, in case we had trouble with the police. I could tell he was angry, but I was in charge.

We weren't waiting long before Chuck radioed to tell us that the drugstore was closed. I went up first to make sure no one had disturbed our work. Everything looked good, so I called my brother and Broeckels up to join me. We reopened the hole and climbed back into the vault. Before long, we were back to punching out locks with the B&O.

As we moved down the line breaking locks, I told Broeckels to pull out the boxes and look for valuables. We had finished off the large and medium boxes the night before. All that was left were the small safety deposit boxes. Those usually held cash.

Broeckels' job was easy, but he kept stopping to show us the strange stuff he found.

"We don't have time for this," I finally said. "You know what to look for. Throw the rest of the shit on the floor." I knew we had to keep moving or we'd run out of time.

It was getting late. I thought we should just load up and go. At that point, we were really just looking for pennies, compared to what we already had. But then I thought about how many thieves in the world would kill to be in a bank vault like this one. We already had the millions we came for, and it was hot as hell, but we kept working as fast as we could. Pretty soon, it became harder and harder to knock out locks. We were getting to the upper rows, and it was hard to swing the sledge so high.

"Forget the rest of the boxes," I said. "It'll be daylight in a couple of hours."

But my brother didn't want to leave anything. "If you're worried about time, we can have Ace pick up the loot behind the bank, okay? Then we won't have to carry all this shit back. Some of the bags are pretty fucking heavy. I don't feel like hauling them to the condo."

"I guess that will work." I was exhausted, so the idea sounded great.

We decided to call Ace about thirty minutes before dawn. As tired as I was, we couldn't chance riding back with him. We would have to walk. If someone saw us getting out of the car looking haggard and suspicious, they would definitely call the police.

Finally we had to give up. The vault looked like a tornado had come through. We had managed to open 458 of the 500 boxes. That was pretty good, I thought. I was proud of the job.

In an article written years after the burglary, FBI agent Jim Conway—the first agent to arrive at the bank vault after the burglary was reported—described his report from the crime scene:

The inside of the vault looks like it has been through a blender. Shredded sandbags, broken concrete, crushed safe-deposit boxes, dumped documents, junked jewelry, even discarded cash fill the room. The debris is, in some places, shoulder-high. It doesn't take a detective to figure out this burglary is different. Two beaten alarm systems, explosives, severed steel rods. This is a heavyweight job. It was sophisticated, something I've never seen before. It is a colossal mess in so many ways. Since the target is safe-deposit boxes, the bank has no record of what is missing. [...] By the first afternoon, the vault turns into an archeological dig, with FBI agents and the bank sifting through the debris.

FBI agent Paul Chamberlin added, "We had more heat on this case than you can shake a stick at. One hundred and twenty-five agents working the case—that is unheard of. It was the biggest commitment of FBI personnel that anybody had ever heard of."

At the time, we were more concerned with getting out of the vault and back to the condo than with how the crime scene looked. I told my brother and Broeckels to go up the ladder to the top of the vault and drop a rope down. Then I tied our loot-filled bags on, and they pulled the bags up. After we had all the bags and tools on the roof, my brother and Broeckels lowered them to Phil on the ground.

Meanwhile, I opened a small stainless steel door built into a cavity in the vault door, where there are three precision-time clocks mounted. I knew a bank employee could set any number of hours or minutes to regulate when the bank would reopen the vault. There are three clocks so that if one malfunctions, there are still two backups. The odds of all three clocks breaking at the same time were infinitesimal.

That night, though, it would happen.

I jammed all three clocks, turned off the vault lights, and went up to the roof. I didn't bother covering the hole. We planned on being long gone by the time the breach was discovered.

Down on the blacktop, I told my brother what I had done to the vault door's three clocks. No one would be opening the vault on time this morning.

"Good," my brother said. "They won't suspect shit."

That's just what happened. When a bank employee tried to open the vault door on Monday morning, it wouldn't budge. The bank called a locksmith, but the locksmith said he couldn't come until that afternoon. Not thinking anything of it, the bank manager borrowed money from one of the bank's other branches. They opened for business as usual.

When the locksmith finally arrived, he spent several hours attempting to get the door open. He couldn't get through. Finally, he told the bank manager that he would have to make a hole in the concrete vault to open the door. When he lifted a drop ceiling tile to get on top of the vault, he saw that someone had already made a hole.

By that time, we were back at the condo cleaning up. At dawn, Ace had picked up the loot and tools. He took them back to the condo while my brother, Chuck, Phil, Broeckels, and I walked back.

I didn't want Phil or Broeckels to know we were taking the loot to Ace's garage. Once we were back at the condo, I told them Ace was going to take my brother, the loot, and me to a friend's house in Pasadena. I said we would hide it there for a few days.

Before we left, I told Chuck, Phil, and Broeckels to clean up and pack their suitcases. When Ace got back, he would take Phil and Broeckels to the airport. Meanwhile, Chuck would keep wiping down the condo until my brother and I came back to get him.

We had loot and burglar tools in the trunk of the blow car, and there was no way I was going to unload and sort through that stuff at the condo. I wanted to clear out of the area as quickly as possible. I gave Phil two thousand dollars and told him and Broeckels that I would see them back in Ohio in a week. My brother and I drove Ronnie's car. It was exhilarating driving, knowing that Tricky Dick's money was in the trunk. Ace drove the blow car. Once we were at Ace's house, we unloaded the loot and tools. We stashed the loot in the garage and put the tools back in the false bottom of the blow car.

I was anxious to get Nixon's money out of the trunk without Ace seeing it, since I hadn't told him or Ronnie anything about it. So when Ace left to take Phil and Broeckels to the airport, my brother and I hid the money behind an old rug at the back of the garage.

Next, we headed to the condo in Ronnie's car. When we got there, Ace had already picked up Phil and Broeckels. Chuck was wiping down the place and listening to the police scanners. So far, there had been no mention of the bank burglary.

While Chuck and my brother finished up, I took a ride over to check out the bank. From the parkway, I could see the hole in the roof and the ladder sticking up out of the hole—just like we had left it. I knew that if the bank employees suspected anything, there would be police all around the bank. My trick with the vault door timers must have worked. It was almost noon. People were walking in and out of the bank as usual. We were in the clear.

I headed back to the condo. When Ace returned from the airport, I told him to follow Chuck in Ronnie's car. My brother-in-law was taking the blow car to the home of a friend of his, Earl Dawson, who had agreed to store it for us. Chuck would need a ride back. By the time they returned, my brother and I had turned on the dishwasher and finished cleaning the condo. We all headed over to Ace's house and caught a few hours of sleep.

After waking up and taking a nice, hot shower, I told everyone to start counting the cash. We could leave the gold, jewelry, and bonds until we reached Ohio, but I needed to know how much cash we were going to have laundered in Vegas.

My brother agreed that we should get on the road as soon as possible. After deciding we'd head out early the next morning, I went to the supermarket to buy some food. I found a broiler with ten whole chickens turning on spits. I told the lady behind the counter to wrap all of them up for me. She laughed and asked if I was hungry.

"Like a grizzly bear," I said. It felt good to flirt a little. I was high on the fact that no one knew what we had just done.

When I got back to Ace's house, my brother, Chuck, and Ace were counting the money. We took a break to eat and then finished counting. We kept the scanners and television on to see if there was any word on the robbery. Nothing caught our attention. Chuck thought the burglary might have been discovered while we were sleeping, but I told him that wasn't likely. If the burglary had been exposed, it would be all over the news.

Once the money was all counted, we found we had just over eight hundred thousand dollars for three nights of work. From the looks of the homes in the area, I thought there should have been much more cash. But we still had the gold coins, jewelry, stocks, and bonds to go through. I knew those would add up to a tidy sum.

We put all the gold and other coins in garbage bags, doubling the bags to keep them strong. Then we settled the bags in the suitcases. We did the same with the jewelry, but left the stocks and bonds in the burlap feed sacks.

That night, there was a story on the news about the burglary. We all leaned forward to listen. The bank manager discussed the looting of the safety deposit boxes. He said that the FBI and Orange County Sheriff's Office were investigating. He acted like it wasn't a big deal. We knew better.

On Tuesday morning, Chuck took the blow driver's license we had used to buy the blow car and rented a small U-Haul truck. While loading the loot, I managed to pack in Tricky Dick's money without Ace noticing. When the truck was loaded, we were on our way to Las Vegas. Chuck drove the truck. My brother, Ace, and I followed in Ronnie's car.

"No matter what, don't speed," I warned Chuck. He assured me that he wouldn't.

Meanwhile, the Laguna Niguel bank burglary dominated the news. It was the biggest story in the country. That is, until June 17, 1972, when a seemingly small-time break-in at the Watergate Hotel started making headlines.

CHAPTER EIGHT

The Loot in Las Vegas

We arrived in Vegas at around two o'clock in the afternoon. I called my friend Joey from a phone booth outside a small restaurant. I knew Joey had mafia connections that could launder big bills, so I was desperate to get in touch with him. The phone rang and rang but there was no answer. I slammed down the receiver in frustration.

Across the street was a Holiday Inn. I told Chuck to rent two connecting rooms. After some discussion, we decided to rent a set of wheels, too, and let Ace drive Ronnie's car back to California.

My brother took a cab to the airport and chose a shiny Ford LTD. The model has a huge trunk, which was perfect for our purposes. After Ace left, Chuck, my brother, and I carried Nixon's money into the motel room to count it. There were seven thousand thousand-dollar bills and eight thousand five-hundred-dollar bills. That added up to a total of eleven million dollars. There was also the one million in new one-hundred-dollar bills. In the end, we had stolen twelve million bucks from the President of the United States.

Even today, I get chills thinking about that moment.

Later that evening, I tried Joey again. This time, a woman told me Joey was working. Figuring he would be at the casino, I called a cab. Before I left, I made sure to tell my brother and Chuck to keep an eye on our U-Haul. The last thing we wanted was our score getting ripped off from the motel parking lot.

On the ride to the casino, I pictured how Joey would react when I told him how much cash I needed laundered. I knew he was going to have a fit. That would be hilarious to watch, but the bad side was that his connections might not want to handle such big bills. Even worse, they might charge more than the usual 3 percent. I didn't know what I would do if they tried to charge more for the service fee. I figured my brother and I might just have to hang on to the larger bills.

I knew my friend was only the middleman and that the big boys at the casino no doubt liked to make free money, but all they really did was take in our big bills and give back clean one-hundred-dollar bills. It didn't cost them a red cent. There was no way I was going to pay out the nose for that. I decided that if they got greedy, I would find another way. As I had told my brother, this loot was already getting split too many ways, especially once we factored in paying off Butchie, his source, and Hoffa.

I found Joey quickly at the casino. He worked as a pit boss in the craps table area. As soon as I walked into his area, I immediately spotted him looming over the betting action. When he spotted me, he motioned for someone to take his place and strolled over to shake my hand.

"Is there somewhere else we can talk?" I asked. The place was swarming with people.

Joey led me into some kind of private lounge. A waitress rushed over and immediately took our drink orders. When we were settled, Joey asked why I was back in town again so soon.

"Business," I said. "Listen, Joey. This is serious." I told him that I had money to wash. When he asked how much, I quoted the figure. He just sat there for a few seconds saying nothing. His jaw was slack and his eyes darted all over my face, trying to read whether I was serious.

When he could finally speak, he said, "What the hell did you do, rob a Federal Reserve Bank or some shit?"

"I wish," I said, smiling. "No, man. I just got lucky. So what do you think? Can your friend handle that much cash?"

Joey scratched his head. I could tell he hadn't been expecting anything this dramatic to happen on his shift. "I'm sure he can, but not all at once. I don't know. It would probably take a few days, I guess. The casino only keeps about three million on hand at any given time. What denominations are we talking about here? Would you want C-notes?"

"Yeah," I said. I explained that I had one million in new one-hundred-dollar bills with serial numbers in sequence and a Dallas Federal Reserve Bank Seal, as well as eleven million in five-hundred- and one-thousand-dollar bills with old and new bills mixed together. Finally, I told him about the eight hundred thousand dollars in mixed small bills.

All of this made Joey nervous. He twitched on his seat and looked around to make sure no one was watching us. I was afraid he thought I might be trying to set him up or something, so I assured him that all of the money came from safety deposit boxes in a bank vault.

"Look, man," I said. "You don't have to worry about the new C-notes or the larger bills. Just get the other stuff clean." I paused, tracking his expression. "Do you think I'm trying to set you up or something?"

"No way," he said, waving his hands. "Of course not. I just don't know if my guy will handle the large bills. There aren't too many of those around anymore. I'll have to talk to him." He leaned back and snickered, shaking his head. "Man, I can't believe some of the things you come up with. How the hell did you find a bank vault with that much cash in the fucking safety deposit boxes?"

"It's a really long story," I said. "Like I said, I got lucky."

"That's why you borrowed my car, right?" Joey leaned back against the couch like he had figured it all out. Little did he know whose money we were talking about.

"Bingo," I said, giving him the satisfaction. I knew he would eventually hear about the burglary, but I didn't care. At that moment, all I wanted was the clean bills.

I told him if his friend could handle the money, I would give him twenty thousand dollars as well as an additional ten thousand for having used his car. I figured that would perk him up.

"If your friend can't handle the big bills, I'll take them to another connection." Joey knew that I was acquainted with a few mob guys, and I wanted him to think I had plenty of options. But really I was just bluffing. I didn't have a mafia guy that I would trust with twelve million, but there was no way I was going to tell Joey that. I wanted to push him to give me a fair rate, even though I was starting to realize he was gearing up to ask for some serious cash for the job.

"Let me talk to my friend. I'll get back to you." He ran a hand through his hair. "How about we meet here at one o'clock tomorrow?"

I agreed. Now that our business was settled for the moment, he asked how things were going in Youngstown.

"You know how it is," I said. "Shit never gets better. That town went to the dogs a long time ago."

"Why don't you move out here?" he asked. "I could hook you up with a good gig."

That made me laugh out loud. One of the waitresses looked over. "Maybe," I said, "If I believed in paychecks or paying taxes. Besides, man, my family is in Ohio. I'm cursed to die in that fucking town."

Joey just laughed. After he signed the tab, we went our separate ways.

Outside the casino, I flagged a cab and headed back to the motel. As we shot down the highway, I thought about the fact that this job could end up taking several days. That left us sitting in the middle of Las Vegas with a U-Haul truck full of stolen money parked in a motel lot. I knew motel lots were often targets for break-ins. Moreover, we sure as hell couldn't sit around in the same room day after day. Someone at the hotel was bound to get suspicious.

After arriving back at the motel, I updated my brother and Chuck on what Joey had said. I told them the bad news and said that if Joey's friend refused to take the large bills or charged us a huge fee, we'd have to take them back to Ohio with us.

"What the hell do we do with all those bills in Ohio?" my brother asked.

"That's a question that I don't have an answer to at the moment. We'll just have to keep them hidden until we figure out what to do. The good thing is that I don't think the FBI will be looking for them. Think about it. There's no way Tricky Dick reported them stolen. That would be roasting his own ass. And we know plenty of crooks, right? I'm sure we'll figure something out. Let's just wait and see what Joey's guy says."

I picked up a pencil and tablet from the nightstand and worked out some calculations. We had eleven million in five-hundred- and one-thousand-dollar bills and another one million in new one-hundred-dollar bills, besides the eight hundred thousand from the other safety deposit boxes and the bank's operating money. At 3 percent to launder the money, that would cost us approximately $384,000. As for the guys in the casino, they would be making a tax-free income of three hundred and eighty thousand. Back in 1972, that was big money. The fact that they could make money so easily off of our hard work and all the risks we had taken just irritated me. I couldn't let go of that.

As we sat around sharing thoughts, I suggested to my brother and Chuck that we could reduce the $384,000 fee if we gave Hoffa his 5 percent out of the five-hundred- and one-thousand-dollar bills. After all, why pay to have his share laundered? And that would still mean that Hoffa got his six hundred thousand. In working it out this way, I figured we could save eighteen thousand on the laundering fee, which wasn't nothing. We separated out three hundred thousand dollars in five-hundred-dollar bills and three hundred thousand in one-thousand-dollar bills and set it all over on a small table. That money was for Hoffa. That left us with $11,400,000. At 3 percent for the fee, the total we would pay came to $342,000. We still also had the eight hundred thousand, which would cost us another twenty-four thousand to launder. The grand total would be $366,000 to get back clean money.

I reminded my brother and Chuck that we still had some other expenses. We hadn't paid off Butchie, BB, or BB's friend in Detroit. Butchie had given us a great lead on the score, so I wanted to take good care of him. We wouldn't have been able to do anything without him. I asked my brother and Chuck what they thought was fair for those guys. They both said it was up to me.

I thought about the situation carefully. If we gave Butchie a million and a half to cover him, BB, and BB's friend, we would still have $9,900,000 left for us to chop up, which would be about $3,300,000 apiece. Of course, that didn't include the eight hundred thousand from the boxes, the gold and silver coins, the jewelry, and the stocks and bonds. All of that miscellany would all add up to a nice piece of money, too. The eight hundred thousand wouldn't be all ours, though. We still had to divide that up with Phil, Broeckels, and Ace, and take good care of Ronnie. I set out this proposal to my brother and Chuck. They agreed to everything. We had a plan.

We briefly discussed pulling one over on Hoffa by claiming there was actually less cash in Tricky Dick's boxes. But after some deliberation, we decided that was a bad idea. If Hoffa ever found out we had cheated him, we would be dead in the street.

"We have to be honest thieves," I reminded my brother and Chuck. "Even though sometimes that hurts."

Although we had some of the loot in the room with us, a good chunk of it was still hidden in the truck outside. I didn't feel comfortable leaving it out there, so that night, I went out and removed the rotor. We didn't want any petty thieves stealing the loot we had rightfully stolen first.

The next day, I met with Joey as planned. He told me his friend would handle the new C-notes for the usual 3 percent, but for the big bills he wanted 8 percent. His reasoning was that those bills would be harder to move through the casino disguised as money taken in from gamblers. I knew there would be a hitch. I told Joey that price was too much.

"I understand your point," Joey said. "If I could do it myself, I'd work for nothing."

I knew that was a lie. He asked if the money was here in town. I was immediately suspicious of the question, and sat up in my seat. I had to be on guard, so I told him that the money wasn't here, but that I could have it in a day. I may not have known much about Joey's alleged "friend," but I was sure I didn't want him to know where we had stashed the loot. I didn't want anyone prowling around our hotel sniffing out the cash. I knew Joey was acquainted with thieves and hit men who would shoot all three of us down for a lot less than twelve million. Joey was a good friend of mine, but with the amount of money I was dealing with, I needed to be extra careful.

I told Joey that I'd call my brother and discuss the 8 percent. Then, I asked if I could bring him the million in new C-notes and the eight hundred thousand in mixed bills, just so we could get that out of the way. He agreed and asked when I could bring it in. I told him I could have it tomorrow.

I made sure no one followed me out of the casino. I didn't notice anyone suspicious, but just to make sure, I went into another casino and walked around inside for a while before catching a cab back to the motel. Once home, I updated my brother and Chuck on everything Joey and I had discussed.

"What are we going to do?" my brother asked when he heard about the 8 percent.

I told him it would be nice to have all the big bills exchanged for C-notes, but the fee was so high that we might as well just haul them back to Ohio and figure out how to move them ourselves once we got there.

But I couldn't stop thinking about the problem. After a lot of deliberation, I finally told myself to forget about Joey's idiot connections. They thought they had me stretched over a barrel with my hands tied, but I wasn't going to roll over for their outrageous 8 percent. I decided I would offer four hundred and fifty thousand to launder all the big bills, including the six hundred thousand we laid aside for Hoffa. If they didn't accept our generous offer, we would just take the money back to Ohio.

In the morning, I told James and Chuck what I had decided. They both agreed that it was a good plan. I took the one million in new one-hundred-dollar bills and the eight hundred thousand in mixed bills to Joey at the casino. He told me to come back at nine o'clock when the job would be done. Then he asked me what I had decided about the big bills.

"Let's get this money taken care of first," I said. I wanted to keep it simple for now.

That night, my brother and I went to pick up the money. It was made up of one-hundred-dollar bills in banded ten-thousand-dollar packets. I gave one pack to Joey, telling him it was payment for letting us use his car. I could see he was surprised, but he just thanked me and slid the money into his hip pocket.

When he had settled the money away, I told him that I had talked his friend's proposition over with my brother and we had decided that we couldn't go for the 8 percent. The quote was just way too much. I said we were willing to pay four hundred and fifty thousand for the laundering. I told him that was my final offer. He could take it or leave it.

Joey slit his eyes and glanced away. I could tell he wasn't impressed. "I know my guy will never go for that, but I'll pass the message on." We arranged to meet in the lounge an hour later.

I met my brother in the casino's waiting area. It felt strange to sit there with nearly $1,750,000 in a suitcase at our feet. I couldn't sit still, couldn't stop thinking about the money down there, wondering if people who walked by could tell something was going on. Finally, Joey returned.

"They can't accept the offer," he said.

"Fine," I said. I tried hard to control my annoyance. "I think they're passing up a generous deal, though. I'm sure something like this won't come up again for a while." I reached out to shake his hand. "We better get moving now." I stood up.

"Wait," Joey said. "Let me try again."

I knew then that Joey's friend would take what he could get. He thought he had us against a wall, but now that his pressure hadn't worked, he was happy to cave. I told Joey we were running late and I didn't know if we had time for him to check with his friend again. I figured I might as well put the pressure on as much as I could.

"Just hold on," Joey said. "I'll be back in twenty minutes." He hurried out of the lounge.

In the end, Joey's friend agreed to launder the big bills for the four hundred and fifty thousand. He demanded a week to do it. My brother and I ended up keeping three hundred of the new five-hundred-dollar bills and three hundred of the new one-thousand-dollar bills for ourselves.

When we were ready to leave Vegas, Chuck rented another U-Haul in his real name. We bought up some cheap furniture and stacked it in the bed of the Ford truck. Driving back to Ohio, we looked just like any other family moving across the country.

Chapter Nine

Robber's Roost

We arrived back in Ohio around April 12. Finally leaving behind the diesel fumes of those big 18-wheelers was a good feeling. After exiting the turnpike, we headed straight to our farm, which we had named "Robbers' Roost." We bought the property under a bogus name in 1961, paying in cash so it could never be traced back to us. If that place could talk, our skins would be cooked for sure.

We had an older man living on the property as a caretaker. We paid him, bought his food, and gave him money to pay our household bills. We also had two dogs from the pound that served as a security system. One was a German shepherd named Joe, and the other was a mixture of a spitz and Chow Chow whom we named Teddy. If Joe and Teddy didn't know you, they would tear you to pieces for so much as setting foot on that land. Both dogs were loyal and fearsome friends.

The farm was perfect for our business as long as the FBI or the Sheriff's Department never knew about it. The house, barn, and a couple of old grain sheds sat at the end of the long driveway. The barn was huge and had a dry dirt floor. Buried under that floor were several large plastic garbage cans. They were the perfect place to stash the loot from the bank burglary. There was nothing better than the feeling we got dropping that money in those bins and knowing Tricky Dick's millions were safe now at last.

Tricky Dick's millions weren't all the loot, though. The next step was to add up the amount for all the bonds. Just as we were getting started, my brother snapped the rubber band off a bundle of bonds. Stuck in between the notes was a white envelope with handwriting that read, "Open after my death." My brother tore open the envelope. He pulled out a confession written by a man who had killed his wife's brother. The author didn't say why he had done it, but he begged for forgiveness.

"I'll bet this guy is pretty fucking worried right now," my brother said.

"Yeah," I said. "I would be if I were him."

We joked about blackmailing the guy, but we would never stoop so low. We tore up the confession and flushed it down the toilet.

Once we had counted all the bonds and buried the loot, I told Chuck to take the rental truck and wait for my brother and me at a nearby truck stop while we went to my brother's house to pick up a car. That way we could return the rental truck and the car to Cleveland. I thought while I was in Cleveland I could give Butchie a call. I never did, though. We were so tired that we just headed back to Youngstown to see our families and rest up.

When I walked into my house, my precious little girls, Melissa and Amie-Jo, ran up to greet me. I was so happy to see them that I couldn't stop hugging and kissing them. They were more beautiful even than I had remembered. I gave my wife a long kiss, whispering in her ear, "Guess who got Tricky Dick's cash?"

She smiled. "I know you did, because you're not pissed off."

Linda had lived with me for years. She knew what I did to make money. I was always honest with her. She also knew me well enough to know that if I had missed my target or if there had been a rumble with the police, I would have come home in a foul mood.

I was pretty tough to live with for a few days after a failed score. But I couldn't imagine failure now. That was the furthest thing from my mind. I smiled back and gave her another kiss.

After an enjoyable night at home, I woke up the next morning at five o'clock. I got dressed and kissed my wife goodbye. She was sad for me to leave again so soon, but there was still unfinished business. I went out to my detached garage and fired up my Jeep. I picked up my brother and we drove to a Howard Johnson's on Market Street to grab something to eat.

As soon as I walked in the door, I saw Lenny Strollo, one of the local mob bosses in town.

"I haven't seen you at the game lately," he said, not even bothering with pleasantries.

"Yeah," I said, "I got a touch of the flu from my girls. I've been pretty laid up."

From the grin on his face, I could tell he didn't believe me for a second. I didn't care, though. There was no way I was telling him where we'd actually been.

After my brother and I finished eating, we decided I would go and see Butchie to make arrangements for handing over Hoffa's money. While I did that, my brother and Chuck would go to the farm to count the gold and other coins and then add up the total cash value of the government bonds.

My brother borrowed my Jeep and dropped me off at my house. I barely had time to say hello again before I grabbed my Oldsmobile and headed for the turnpike. Before getting on the pike, I called Butchie and told him that I would meet him in the parking lot at the Blue Grass Lounge, a local mafia-operated hangout.

I was already waiting in the lot when Butchie arrived. He pulled up alongside my car and told me to follow him. He didn't want to talk at the Blue Grass because of all the ears around there. I trailed him to an alleyway behind a bakery. Getting out of our cars, we gave each other a real Italian embrace and then went in a back door of the bakery. He said hello to a couple of men and several women who were molding pastries from floury hunks of dough. Then we went back to a small office. As soon as we were settled, it was time to talk business.

"You got Tricky Dick's cash?" he asked.

"Did you ever doubt me?" I smiled.

"I knew you'd get it." He was excited. "Fuck. You're one determined guy."

I was nervous to tell him there was only twelve million in the boxes, instead of the thirty million he'd been told there was. But he didn't seem worried at the news.

"That's still good, right?" Butchie asked.

"I'm happy with it," I said. "I just hope Hoffa doesn't think we're fucking with him."

"Don't worry about that. If that's all there was, that's all there was. Hoffa will understand."

After some dickering over the amount of money he should get, we agreed that I'd give him $1,100,000 and he would take care of BB and BB's friend in Detroit. That saved us four hundred thousand, because my original plan was to give Butchie a million and a half. A tipster on a good score usually gets 10 percent for the tip. Looking at it that way, Butchie was getting a good deal. I didn't know how much Butchie was planning to give BB and his friend in Detroit, but the fact was that I really didn't care. Whatever he decided was his business.

We talked about how the score went down. He asked if Phil or Broeckels ever got a glimpse of Nixon's money.

"Hell, no," I told him. I explained how my brother and I had kept the real haul hidden. Butchie agreed that was a pretty slick trick. He told me that Phil had stopped by and told him all about all the loot we had hauled out of the bank.

"He seemed pretty excited," Butchie said. "I don't think he suspects shit."

While we talked, I started to worry about Hoffa getting his six hundred thousand. I trusted Butchie, but I didn't know who would ferry the money over to Hoffa. What if the haul arrived with bills missing, or what if the whole batch disappeared altogether? Hoffa might think I was trying to cheat him. I didn't know how to broach the subject with Butchie without insulting him. Finally, I just flat out said it. That's more my style than beating around the bush.

"Listen," I said. "I don't know how you plan to give Hoffa his money, but I'm afraid of what will happen if he winds up short. You know he'll have us killed."

"Don't worry," Butchie said, "he'll get the money. No one is going to mess with it." I knew Butchie wouldn't try to cheat me, so I immediately felt better.

Next, we discussed the stocks and bonds. We both agreed that the stocks should be burned, but Butchie said he'd like a chance to move some of the government bonds. Apparently, he had a good connection with a union representative and he could get twenty-five cents on the dollar for them. I promised him I'd look into it and get back to him. That sounded like a pretty good deal to me.

With that important business out of the way, we made plans for him and BB to meet me two days later at a truck stop outside of Youngstown to pick up their money and Hoffa's cut.

That hand-off went over without a hitch. With that final move, the score of the United California Bank in Laguna Niguel was wrapped up. I never felt better.

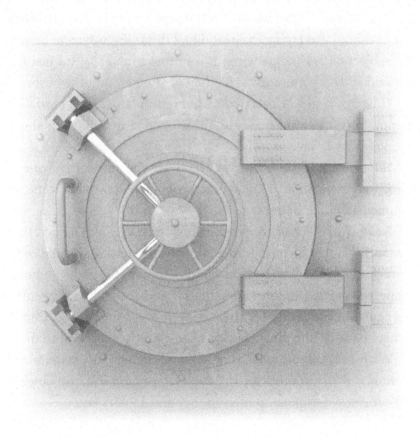

Chapter Ten

Lordstown

After scoring Tricky Dick's cash, everything in my life was running like a dream. I really couldn't have been happier. I was a rich thief with a nice home, a beautiful wife, and two precious little girls. What more could a man ask for? For a guy like me, though, there's always another score waiting around the corner, getting ready to tempt me at any moment.

Towards the end of April, I got a call from an acquaintance named Allen, an ex-detective from Warren, Ohio. I had known him for years, and we had even done some illegal business together when the price was right. Allen wanted more than anything to be involved with the burglary business. He would do everything in his power to make sure a score went off. Once, while helping us out on a jewelry score, he carried the tools to the job in the trunk of the city's detective car. He even let our lookout sit in the car with him while we completed the score.

I knew Allen could have a good tip, so I hurried to meet him at a truck stop just off of Interstate 80. He was all smiles. We discussed a few crimes that had gone down in the area, sharing our opinions on how well the jobs had come off. Then he abruptly asked if I was interested in taking on a three million dollar score.

"Don't you know me?" I said. "Of course I'm up for it."

I wanted to hear the details, though. Much like with the Laguna Niguel job, I was initially suspicious. I had worked with Allen in the past and our scores had come off fine, but just the fact that he was offering me such an easy and giant score smelled like a police trap.

"What's the dirt on the job?" I asked. I decided to evaluate the facts and decide if the score sounded fishy or not.

Allen explained that the target was the Second National Bank of Warren's Lordstown Branch. I was familiar with the building already. I knew it was protected with a Diebold alarm system and had a vault built from eight-inch cement blocks with a half-inch steel liner inside the frame of those blocks. The vault would be really simple to beat because all we had to do was handle the alarm system, which would be no problem, then bust out the cement blocks with a sledgehammer. We would need to use an acetylene-cutting torch to cut through the steel liner, but that wouldn't really be a problem.

Other than featuring a large General Motors automobile assembly plant, Lordstown was a pretty quiet place. There was only one traffic light. If you caught the green light and blinked, you would probably miss the whole town. At night, the police force was nothing more than a constable. After midnight, you couldn't even find him.

Allen went on to explain that on May 4, there would be three million dollars stored in the vault to cover an extra-large GM payroll for workers' bonuses. The money would be delivered on Thursday and paid out on Friday, when the GM workers cashed their payroll checks. For anyone talented enough to pull off the score in a single night, the payoff would be huge.

I tried to stay calm, but my mind was already racing through the logistics. I asked Allen how he got the information. He claimed that an employee from the Second National Bank's main office in downtown Warren, Ohio, told him about the payroll delivery. He said he had known the employee for fifteen years and trusted him. I still thought everything sounded a little fishy. Why would a bank employee be spouting off that kind of information? Especially to Allen, who wasn't the most upstanding citizen? On the other hand, the story sounded plausible. The bank was the only one in town; the factory employees would have nowhere else to cash their checks.

After considering the details, I decided that Allen must be giving me good information. I had never had a problem with tips on scores he had given me in the past. He had always been solid and trustworthy. Plus, the score seemed doable. The bank building was located in a field set off from the highway, with nothing else around. It was an even more ideal situation than in Laguna Niguel. I told him that I'd talk to my brother and take a look at the bank.

The next morning, I told my brother what Allen had said. My brother knew Allen pretty well, too. He asked me what I thought of the score.

"It could be legit," I said. "I've been thinking about it. That GM plant is huge. They employ a shitload of people."

The question was whether we actually wanted to go after the money. We were already fat with millions from the Laguna Niguel burglary, and so there wasn't any urgent reason to take the job. But we both knew that three million dollar scores didn't come along that often, especially when the money was sitting in a bank vault that we knew we could beat in a couple of hours. I knew we would regret not taking the job by the time our funds eventually dried up. The score was just too tempting.

We knew several men and women who worked in the Lordstown GM plant, so we checked out Allen's story by talking to one of them. Sure enough, he told us that Friday was going to be a bonus-sharing payday.

That was just the confirmation we needed.

We decided our first step would be to have a look inside the bank after hours. I got my alarm-checking equipment ready, and Chuck dropped my brother and me off by the bank that very night. We made our way around behind the building and spread out a tarp to sit on while we waited for whatever little traffic there was to die down. Once the shift change at the nearby GM plant had ended, the number of passing cars dwindled to almost nothing. However, the traffic wasn't our real concern. We needed to know if there would be a cleaning crew coming in.

The bank sat back from the highway by about two hundred feet, with no windows facing the road. Bank customers parked in a lot to the left of the building. From there, they entered the bank through two large glass doors. If that lot was full, there was another one in back. There was a single glass door on the back wall of the bank. The vault was at the front of the structure, with its back facing the highway and the big stainless steel vault door facing the back glass door.

Lordstown is so small that it had no police dispatcher. As a result, the Trumbull County Sheriff's Office took all calls for police assistance. The bank's alarm system ran directly through telephone lines to that office. Knowing this, my brother and I programmed the Sheriff's police radio frequency into our portable police scanner. On the night of our stakeout, we listened to the scanner. Hardly any calls came through at all, and not one was more serious than a fender bender.

At three in the morning, I decided it was time to take a look inside the bank. I wanted to read the alarm wires and make sure there was, as I suspected, a Diebold system in place. I sent my brother to keep a look out by the highway so I could safely pick the lock.

After he gave me a 10-4, I peered in the glass door in back.

I could see some dim lights were turned on in the lobby, but I couldn't identify any motion detectors. Believing the coast was clear, I put my miniature flashlight between my teeth and started working on the door lock. The job was simple, and within minutes, I had the door open. I checked the top of the door frame for an alarm contact. There was nothing there.

I stepped inside the bank, savoring that feeling of entering a place you're not supposed to be. I immediately noticed an open door just to the left of the vault door. I crossed the floor to investigate. The door led to a room with a large table and chairs. This must have been the staff break room. I could tell that the right-side wall abutted the left outside wall of the vault. That would be a perfect place to break through.

Next, I found the telephone junction box on the wall in the utility room. Sure enough, there were the two alarm terminals double-capped with red plastic. It was the exact same set-up as in California.

As I explained earlier, the Diebold alarm system operates with DC voltage, so I set my meter on the DC 25-volt reading scale. Removing the red caps from the brass terminals in the junction box, I read the voltage. Next, I used my amplifier to listen to the alarm wires for the line security pulses. That was a giveaway that I was definitely dealing with a Diebold system. Satisfied, I replaced the red caps and shut off the light.

I met my brother back at the highway and told him the system was a Diebold with a pulsar, just like we suspected. Then I clued him in on the break room where we could knock a hole through to the vault.

"Great," he said, excited. "I knew this would be an easy score."

From the highway, the telephone line ran into the bank on wooden poles. The closest pole was forty feet away and had about seven phone lines extending over the roof of the bank to a two-inch steel pipe sticking up about two feet above the roof. The pipe ran down into the utility room to where the telephone junction box was mounted.

My brother and I crouched in the bushes. We figured we would splice into the alarm wires on the roof, then tie in our four-conductor electric cable and extend the alarm wires out from the bank by about three hundred feet into the bushes. There, we would be safe while we hooked in our alarm-bypass box. We always liked to extend the alarm wires out from a bank. That was so we wouldn't be trapped inside if something went wrong during the hookup. You never know what can happen on a score, no matter how good your skills and crew are.

As it turned out, I was right to be careful.

In 1972, Diebold's basic system was pretty simple, though not as simple as the circuit alarm we saw in Laguna Niguel. The main alarm control panel was located in the bank's vault, sending a constant stream of ten to eighteen pulses per second, with 5-8 volts of direct current, over two telephone line wires running between the bank and an alarm-receiving module at the police station. If a bank teller tripped the alarm during a robbery or a burglar set it off at night, the pulses would stop and the receiving module would light up and ring, alerting the police to a problem at the bank. The police would then rush to the bank to find out whether they had a robbery or a false alarm on their hands.

The secret to beating the alarm was to hook into the phone lines coming out of the bank. With them, we could duplicate the ten to eighteen pulses per second without setting off the alarm. We just had to do it without disturbing the pulses transmitting to the police station.

The "boss man" (our alarm-bypassing box) produced the same number of pulses per second as the system transmitting out of the bank. With my four-conductor cable hooked onto the bank's alarm wires and running through the boss man's double-pole micro switch, when we were ready to cut the bank's alarm, all we had to do was flip a switch on the boss man. That stopped the bank's alarm signal at the micro switch and replaced the alarm signal with the pulser built into the boss man. Once we were set up, all we had to do was listen to our police monitor to make sure we had done everything right. If we didn't hear any reports of the bank alarm being triggered, we could go in and pick up our money.

My brother and I spent the next several nights watching the bank. Other than a cleaning crew that came and left before midnight, it was a dead zone.

We prepared to pull off the score on the night of May 4. That was the sweet spot after the payroll money had been delivered on Thursday but before the bank opened up to a flood of eager employees wanting to cash their checks on Friday. Just like in California, we planned to blast a hole through the top of the vault. We figured we could either go through the break room or through the top.

On the night of May 3, Chuck dropped my brother and me off. We filled ten bags with dirt so they weighed about forty pounds each. Then we put them up on the roof of the bank. Once up there, we made a hole in the roof over the top of the vault and laid the bags of dirt on top. The last step was to seal the hole in the roof with tar in case it rained.

Very early on May 4, I had my brother drop me off near the highway. I positioned myself behind the bank in the thick brush with my binoculars ready. I wanted to make sure that the Brink's armored truck actually dropped off the money. A few minutes after ten, the truck pulled up.

A man with a handgun got out of the passenger's side and walked to the truck's back door. He stopped and looked around before knocking. Through my binoculars, I had a direct line of sight. The person inside the truck opened the door and passed out two large white bags, each about three feet long. The armed guard carried both bags to the glass doors. A uniformed security guard let him in.

That's good, I thought. Now, at least we know that there's money in the vault. We wouldn't be too happy if we broke into an empty vault.

That night, my brother, Chuck, and I had a friend drop us off at a dirt driveway five hundred feet up the highway from the bank. We waited until after the shift change at GM. When the traffic had slowed down, we walked through the field to the bank. I had Chuck take a walkie-talkie and a police scanner and sent him out by the highway where he could see up and down the road and could alert us if any cars turned into the bank.

Next, my brother and I climbed an electric conduit up to the roof of the bank. The first thing I did was locate the telephone line carrying the bank's alarm signal to the Sheriff's Office. That was easy enough. I then bared the two copper wires and spliced in our four conductor cable. I checked all the connections to see if they were good. Now we had a three hundred foot loop tied into the bank's alarm system. See pages 155-157.

Using our three-hundred-foot roll of electric cable, we spliced into the bank's alarm system. I wrapped the cable around the two-inch pipe and tied it securely. Meanwhile, my brother lowered himself down to the blacktop. I passed the roll of cable down to him before I headed down myself. Then my brother shimmied up the wooden telephone pole with the cable, all the way to the main telephone cable coming from the highway. He threw the roll over the cable, letting it fall to me. Then I gave it a yank, stretching the wire tight in the air about twenty feet above the ground. I stepped back to observe our work. Our cable looked just like any phone line going from the wooden pole over to the bank.

After my brother came down the pole, we walked away from the bank, unspooling the three hundred feet of cable until we reached a large tree surrounded with heavy bushes and brush. We knew we would be safe there if the alarm bypass failed. See picture of the Lordstown Bank setting in amongst trees, page 160.

I then connected the three hundred foot cable loop onto the four brass bolts (A-B-C-D) on the boss man and made the wire cuts between the brass bolts. Now the bank's alarm was tied into the boss man's double pole micro switch. Then we still had to inject the liquid Styrofoam into the Diebold alarm bell on the outside wall of the bank, which only took about ten minutes. Once that was down, we were ready to replace the alarm signal coming from the bank with the one generated by the boss man.

Using a 12 volt lantern battery, we powered up the boss man. At this point, the bank's alarm signal was still protecting the bank vault and transmitting directly to the Sheriff's Office, but along the way, it was running through the double-pole micro switch inside the boss man.

I radioed Chuck to let him know that I needed him to listen closely to the scanner. Then when he gave me a 10-4, all clear, I flipped the switch on the boss man, which stopped the bank's alarm signal at the double-pole micro switch and cut in our duplicated alarm signal pulses to the Sheriff's Department. Within twenty seconds, Chuck called and said it came over the scanner that there was an alarm drop at the Second National Bank, Lordstown Branch, and a deputy was on his way to the bank.

My shin froze. I couldn't believe it. I knew the connections I had made were good. I knew the boss man was generating a solid pulse, just like the bank's alarm. Something had gone wrong.

I told Chuck to come back where my brother and I were, because if we had to leave we would all be together. We didn't panic. We just hid in the brush and calmly waited for the Sheriff's deputy to arrive. It took a good ten minutes before a cruiser arrived, and soon after another cruiser arrived. Both men got out of their cruisers and shined their flashlights through the bank's windows. They jiggled the door handles, making sure everything was locked.

One of them pulled out his portable police radio and reported to the Sheriff's Office dispatcher that everything looked secure. We heard the crackly voice of the dispatcher say he would call the bank manager for further instructions.

Throughout this entire exchange, my brother, Chuck, and I were less than three hundred feet away. We prayed the police wouldn't notice anything. Less than a minute later, the dispatcher called back and said the bank manager had asked if the alarm bell was ringing. The deputies said it was not, thanks to our careful job. The dispatcher told the police that the bank manager said if the bell wasn't ringing, it was a false alarm. He thought the system must have malfunctioned. The manager promised he would call a repairman in the morning. Crouched in the bushes, I thanked god for the liquid Styrofoam.

My brother, Chuck, and I were stunned into silence as the cruisers drove away. We waited in the brush for another fifteen or twenty minutes, just to be safe. When we were certain the coast was clear, my brother and I wanted to continue as planned. Chuck told us to forget the job. He argued that we had enough money from Laguna Niguel. I knew he was right, but by that time, my brother and I wanted that three million pretty badly. I sent Chuck back to his lookout post.

We did revise our plans, though. My brother and I decided to break into the vault through the break room wall rather than the ceiling. We had less time now, and there was no point in hiding the hole up top anyway. If a repairman was coming tomorrow, he would find the hole wherever it was. It didn't matter how we got into the vault, as long as we had enough time to clear it out.

My brother and I scaled the electric conduit to the bank's roof and opened the hole we had made over the top of the vault. I kicked two or three ceiling tiles down into the room beside the vault and then lowered myself into the break room. My brother handed me the tools we had stored on top of the vault and then followed me down.

We worked fast. While I was hooking up the acetylene-cutting torch and preparing to cut through the half-inch steel vault liner, my brother was sledge-hammering out the eight-inch cement blocks on the side of the vault. He finished in ten minutes, so I lit the cutting torch and went to work slicing a crawl hole. I finished the crawl hole in fifteen minutes, but the steel was so hot that we had to get water from the bathroom to cool it off. Once we had the steel cooled, I crawled into the vault and turned on the light.

I evaluated the scene. To my left was a five-foot-tall double-door square safe. Sitting in front of that was a cart with the bank tellers' money drawers on it, full of cash. But I knew the big money would be inside the safe. That worried me. The safe would take time to figure out how to open, and time was something we didn't have.

Just on a lark, I grabbed the safe's door handle and gave it a hard twist. To my amazement, the door swung open.

I could not believe my eyes. The safe was actually unlocked.

I opened both doors and immediately saw that the shelves were stacked with money. At first, I was filled with excitement at this discovery. But when I started to fill one of my large army duffle bags, I realized the bundles only contained twenty-dollar bills. That didn't seem right to me. If all the cash in this safe was all in twenty-dollar bills, there was no way it could add up to the three million Allen had promised.

After filling the first bag, I handed it through the crawl hole to my brother. He stood on the table and passed it up to the top of the vault while I started filling another bag. The further I got into the safe, though, the smaller the bills became. There were tons of bundles of ten-dollar and even five-dollar bills, with just a few bundles of fifty-dollar and one-hundred-dollar bills mixed in. Down at the bottom, there were even bundles of one-dollar bills. I couldn't believe it.

By the time the second bag was full, the safe was completely cleaned out. I handed the bag out to my brother. I said I was going to look around the vault to see if there was another safe we were missing. I prayed there was, because we sure as hell didn't have three million dollars.

There was nothing else.

After that, I cleaned out the tellers' drawers. I made sure to keep the bait bills separate so I could have them laundered properly later.

Studying the wall of safety deposit boxes, especially the large ones lining the bottom row, I wondered if maybe the bank had stored its larger fifty-dollar and one-hundred-dollar bills in those boxes. But we were running against the clock at this point. I knew there was no way we would have time to open them. We had to get ourselves out of the vault and off the roads before daylight. If the big bills were in a safety deposit box, we would never know.

Once we got all the money out of the vault, I told my brother that most of the cash was in twenty-dollar bills and that we had definitely fallen short of Allen's promise.

"Are you sure?" he asked, looking upset.

"I know money," I said. "We definitely don't have three million here. Maybe five hundred thousand at the most." When we got home and counted the money, the load turned out to be $430,000. That was a good haul for a deposit safe burglary, but not much of a take for a vault score.

The next morning, Allen called to say he was at the doughnut shop on Market. He wanted to see me. At first, I told him I was busy, still angry over the low take. After some cajoling, though, I finally agreed to meet him. I figured I might as well let the idiot know he had lied and that I wasn't too happy about it.

When I walked into the doughnut shop, Allen was all smiles.

I looked at him coldly and didn't smile back.

"I heard on the news that the Lordstown bank was robbed," he jabbered, as soon as I sat down. "The radio said a shit ton of money was stolen."

"Yeah," I replied. "Around four hundred thousand. Where the hell is the three million?"

The smile dropped off Allen's face. "What do you mean?"

"Look," I said, in my most severe tone. "I'll say it again. The vault didn't have three million dollars. There's nothing I hate more than when some idiot makes a fool out of me. Now I'm going to catch all kinds of heat from the FBI over a completely shitty haul." I was really angry. I told him that I didn't buy the story that he had been tipped off to the three million. I thought he just needed some money and knew I'd only go for the score if it was hefty.

"I'd never do that," he protested.

In the end, I gave him twenty-five thousand. I really shouldn't have given him a penny. I also told him to forget my phone number. I heard he died sometime in the 1970s, but I never saw him again.

I had originally planned to haul the money to Vegas so my connections could exchange it. But then I heard that a mafia guy I knew, Pat Ferruccio, was heading to Vegas the following Sunday. His connections had exchanged money for us in the past at the 3 percent rate, so I figured I'd save myself the trip. I asked Ferruccio to take care of the laundering for me. He happily agreed to the job. I really wish he hadn't.

After I handed off the cash, I still had a nagging problem from the Lordstown job. I wanted to figure out why I hadn't been able to bypass the Diebold alarm. I usually can disable alarms without a hitch, so it bothered me that the system had gone off. Knowing I wouldn't get any peace until I figured out what went wrong, I told my brother we needed to return to the bank and read the alarm line wires. My brother thought I was completely insane for wanting to go back there. But I had to know.

The next night, Chuck dropped my brother and me off up the road from the bank around midnight. We snuck through the brush on foot. Keeping our distance, we spent a few hours casing the building to make sure no one was around. At three o'clock, my brother took a walkie-talkie and the police scanner over to the highway to keep watch.

I climbed up to the roof of the bank. The telephone company had strung a new phone line cable from the telephone pole over to the steel pipe that passed through the roof to the utility room. I cut the new cable open. Using the amplifier, I searched through the pairs of phone lines until I found the alarm wires.

The alarm pulses confirmed it was a Diebold alarm, just as I had thought. I set my meter to count the number of pulses per second. The meter showed a steady ten pulses per second instead of the normal fluctuation of anywhere between ten and eighteen pulses. That's when I knew what had happened when I set off the alarm.

Diebold had upgraded their alarm system to make it more sensitive. Those sneaky bastards.

Our boss man was putting out between ten and eighteen pulses per second. When I flipped the switch to cut the bank's alarm, my boss man's pulses were too frequent. That alerted the receiving module that something was wrong. Had I taken a pulse reading the night we beat the vault, I would have never tied in our boss man to the bank's alarm.

We had been very lucky.

When I told my brother what I'd learned, he was surprised. Diebold had been trying to outsmart us. We could easily adjust our equipment, but the incident taught us a valuable lesson. From now on, we had to make sure to read the pulses on every score before we tied in the boss man, even if we thought we knew the alarm system brand cold.

I felt satisfied as we headed home that night. I didn't know yet that we had much bigger problems on the horizon.

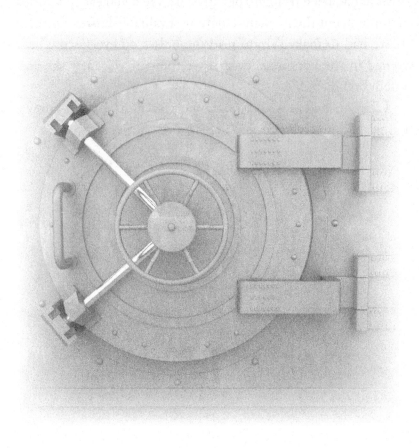

CHAPTER ELEVEN

The Heat Is On

The money I gave Pat Ferruccio to exchange in Las Vegas never even left Ohio. Behind my back, Ferruccio tried to launder the money locally so he could keep the service fee for himself. He handed off the cash to his flunky, Sidney Goldstein, with orders to exchange the bills at various banks in the Canton, Ohio, area. Unfortunately, FBI agents were watching one of the banks Goldstein visited. When Goldstein left the bank, the agents seized the exchanged bills as evidence. The agents then followed him to the other banks where he did the same thing. In his wake, they gathered all the bills to build up a case.

Goldstein was arrested by FBI agents on May 27, 1972, and charged with receiving, possessing, storing, and disposing of money in the amount of one hundred and twenty thousand dollars from the Lordstown bank burglary.

Until Goldstein was arrested, we had no idea the FBI had been keeping tabs on his exchanges. After his arrest, we knew the heat was on us. I was really pissed off that Ferruccio had lied to me about taking the money to Vegas. Ferruccio was worth millions. He didn't need the 3 percent exchange rate, which would have only amounted to around twelve thousand dollars. That just goes to show that you can't trust a mafia boss.

Even before I found out what Ferruccio had done, I was worried something might go wrong. Following my instincts, I decided to take some precautions. This was back in April, over a month before Goldstein was arrested. I had one hundred and sixty thousand dollars hidden in my house. I was getting nervous about having so much cash just lying around, so I took one hundred and twenty thousand in fifty-, one-hundred-, five-hundred-, and one-thousand-dollar bills and stuffed it all in a plastic waterproof picnic jug. Then I buried the jug in my neighbor's front yard, digging the hole in the middle of the night under a looming pine tree.

When my brother and I realized the FBI had been watching Goldstein, we started to worry that the FBI might be watching us, too. But all we could do was sit tight and see what happened next. The fact was that I didn't even feel safe trying to dig up my security money. We knew the feds were likely tapping our telephones, so we became very careful about what we said over the line. After a while had passed where nothing happened, though, we started to wonder if we really did have anything to worry about. Sure, the feds had Goldstein and might be watching us, but there was no way they had anything connecting us to Lordstown. We had been so careful.

When I asked Ferruccio if he thought Goldstein would keep his mouth shut, he told me not to worry. "There's no way in hell Sid's going to talk," Ferruccio promised. "He's not going to prison, either. I'll have the case kicked around in Cleveland. Sid will get probation at the worst."

That's just what happened. On April 23, 1974, Goldstein changed his not guilty plea to guilty. He received five years' probation from Federal Judge Frank Battisti, a judge the Cleveland mafia had kept in its pocket for years.

I would not be so lucky.

On June 1, 1972, while I was having lunch in a local Howard Johnson's, a Mahoning County Sheriff's Office detective came over and sat down with me. I had known him for years, but I figured he couldn't be bearing good news. I was right. After talking for a while, the detective asked if I had been in California lately. I said I hadn't.

"Well, your name is being kicked around out there," he said. "You should look into it, if you know what's good for you."

The detective just leaned back and smiled. I felt my stomach drop. As far as I knew, there was nothing connecting us to California. I thanked him for the tip. He left, but I couldn't shake the feeling that I was being watched. Deciding I needed to take some precautions, I called Chuck up and told him to meet me. When he arrived, I filled him in on everything the detective had said. We both agreed that something must be wrong in California.

Had the FBI found the car? We knew that Chuck's old Marine buddy, Earl Dawson, was keeping it at his house for us, so it should have been safe. But we decided that Chuck should fly to California and burn the car with all our tools still inside.

On June 2, Chuck bought an airline ticket for Los Angeles. While he was at the airport, he called Earl to tell him he was on his way over. According to later FBI statements, an agent, Francis Calley, was already at the Dawson's residence when Chuck called. Apparently, Earl gave him permission to listen in on the conversation. Agent Calley claimed that he told Earl to have Chuck meet him at the Walnut Room, a bar not far from Earl's home in Tustin, CA. Chuck didn't even know what he was walking into.

When Chuck arrived in Los Angeles, he took a cab straight to the Walnut Room. Instead of finding Earl, he was ambushed and arrested by fifteen FBI agents.

According to the FBI, June 2 was the first time they had been to the Dawson's residence and the first time they had seen the

1962 Oldsmobile. On that same day, at eight o'clock, they claimed they obtained a search warrant to search the car in Earl Dawson's garage. They said they found the tools used to burglarize the United California Bank vault at Laguna Niguel in the trunk of the car, including flashlights and a shotgun.

All of this is according to FBI statements. In my opinion, the reality of what happened was much different. I believe that the FBI did not want Chuck to get anywhere near Earl's house. If he had, he would have seen that the car was missing. Using evidence that has come to light since the trial, I realized that the FBI had, in reality, searched the car several days earlier, without a warrant. They seized the vehicle, and only then, using fabricated evidence, received a warrant for June 2. I wouldn't learn of any of this until much too late.

I knew Chuck was solid as steel and wasn't going to give the FBI the right time of day, let alone the details of the score. But I also knew we had a very big problem. Chuck's name was appearing in every newspaper from *The Los Angeles Times* to *The Youngstown Vindicator*. The television news was covering the story relentlessly. All hell had broken loose.

My wife flew out to California to visit Chuck, her brother, in the county jail. While there, she hired him an attorney. I hung around at home and tried to keep my regular routine. I am certain I was followed every minute of that time.

I was in trouble, because I knew I needed some monetary security, but I was afraid to dig up the one hundred and twenty thousand or go out to our farm to get some other money. I figured the FBI was lurking somewhere nearby. No matter how careful I was, they would find some way to trail me.

It probably didn't matter in the end, anyway. There probably wasn't much I could have done to stop what was about to happen. The whole case was already rolling ahead like an out of control snowball.

On June 27, 1972, I left my home at around seven-thirty in the morning. I had only driven about five hundred feet up the street when I noticed two black cars leaving my neighbor's driveway. With red and blue lights flashing, they were coming up fast behind me. Just as they got near, a few more pulled up from a side street. I stopped the car. My throat started to close up. This wasn't good.

One FBI car slid in fast in front of my car, blocking me from moving. A few other agents emerged from their cars with guns drawn.

"Amil Dinsio," one agent called out. "This is the FBI. You're under arrest. Put your hands up."

I did what he said. My hands were handcuffed behind my back while an agent searched me. When he took money from my pocket and put it in his own, I told him to stop.

"Hey," I said. "What the hell are you doing? My money is not a weapon. Put that back. I don't want you guys planting any fucking bait money on me."

"We wouldn't do that," A red-haired agent protested. I knew otherwise, though I didn't yet know the sheer depth of their corruption.

"Before that money leaves my sight, I want a list of the serial numbers. I know exactly what you assholes are capable of." The agent who took the money out of my pocket sheepishly put it back.

"Dinsio doesn't trust us," another agent joked. Several others laughed.

I was taken to the FBI's office in Austintown, a suburb west of Youngstown. The agents released my handcuffs and I sat on one side of a table with an agent facing me and counting my pocket money. After the money was counted, he took each bill and wrote down the serial numbers. As he recorded the numbers, I double-checked them with the bills. I wasn't about to give the agent any kind of opportunity. Even then, I knew how crooked the feds could be. Still, I didn't yet know just how far they would go. After the serial numbers were recorded, I was fingerprinted, photographed, and driven to Cleveland to be booked into the Cuyahoga County Jail.

That same afternoon, thirty FBI agents converged on my home with a search warrant to comb my house and detached garage. Years later, I would find out that the FBI agents had burglarized that same garage before that day to steal a battery with my fingerprint on it. The government would use the stolen flashlight battery as probable cause in the search warrant's affidavit. That's the honest government at work for you.

At the time of my arrest, a federal grand jury judge in Los Angeles set my bail at one million dollars. I had my wife hire attorney Carmon Policy in Youngstown. With connections to federal judges in Cleveland, I hoped he could get the bail reduced so I could travel to California for my arraignment of my own volition as a sign of good faith. He told me he would see what he could do.

When we appeared before Judge Manos in Cleveland to ask for the bail to be reduced to fifty thousand dollars, the FBI blindsided me. With two Federal Marshals guarding me, and Timothy Potts arguing for the U.S. Attorney's Office, the Cleveland judge called the California judge on speakerphone and told him what was going on. Before my attorney could even say anything, the California judge revealed that it had been brought to his attention that one of my neighbor's kids had seen me bury something in their yard. The kid apparently dug it up and found one hundred thousand dollars. When he handed the cash to his mother, she called the FBI.

I knew then that the FBI had seen me bury the money, and not any little neighbor boy sleeping on a porch. I also knew the money was clean and couldn't be connected to the California bank burglary. I didn't have anything to worry about. Losing one hundred and twenty grand wouldn't break me, and the one-thousand- and five-hundred-dollar bills in the jug had come from the gamblers' money betting at the barbotte game. Besides, I knew that there was no way in hell Tricky Dick was going to be crying to the government that those big bills were stolen from him.

After hanging up with the judge in California, Judge Manos denied me bail reduction. The U.S. Marshals took me back to the county jail. Within in a day or two, I was on my way to the Los Angeles County Jail.

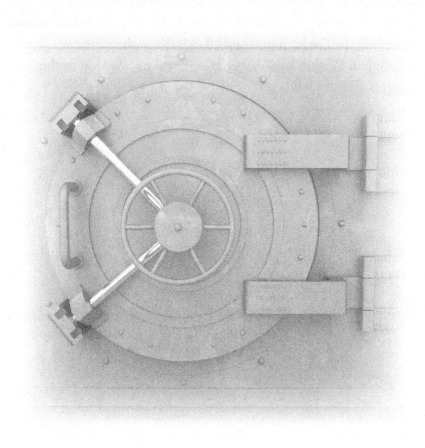

CHAPTER TWELVE

The Frame-up

After I was remanded at the Los Angeles County Jail, Linda flew out to see me. She hired me a fancy Beverly Hills lawyer named Victor Sherman. Most importantly, she brought me the FBI search warrants for my home and the 1962 Oldsmobile. As soon as I read the warrants, I knew something was wrong.

The first obvious problem, a sign that the feds were planting evidence, was a statement claiming that a flashlight battery with my fingerprints on it was found in the false trunk of the car with our other tools. I knew for sure that my fingerprints couldn't have been on any battery inside the trunk. The FBI must have stolen a battery from one of my home garages or from the garbage. I also considered the possibility that agents may have lifted one of my fingerprints from a prior arrest record card and photographed it onto a battery in the FBI laboratory. That sounds like an extreme tactic, but I wouldn't put underhanded methods like that past the feds, not for a second.

The second item I noticed on the warrant was a claim that three gold coins had been found in the car's false bottom. These coins would be identified during the trial as having been stolen from a safety deposit box during the Laguna bank burglary. The coins immediately sounded fishy to me. We had cleaned out that car from top to bottom. There was no way anything had been left behind. Fabricating that evidence would have been easy enough, since the FBI had a large pile of valuables from the safety deposits in the bank vault. All the agents had to do was plant a few outstanding coins in the car.

The pattern of planted evidence and harassment didn't end with me. The feds went after my family as well. During the search of my home, FBI agent John Roberson grabbed my mother-in-law's purse.

"Mrs. Mulligan," he said, before he even looked in the bag. "You are in big trouble." He rifled through the purse and finally pulled out an envelope that had "apartment rent money" clearly printed on the front. Then he fingered through the cash until he found a twenty-dollar bill. Pretending to study it, he told her that the serial number matched a bait bill that had been stolen during the Laguna Niguel burglary.

"If you tell me that Amil gave you this money, I won't arrest you."

My mother-in-law stood her ground. She told him that the money was for her rent, which was the truth. Making good on his threat, Roberson immediately arrested her. She was taken before a federal magistrate and released on a fifty-thousand-dollar bail. Luckily, the charges were eventually dismissed, but this incident was evidence of the kind of corruption and persecution my family was facing.

Roberson went on to claim that he had found a "gold-plated silver dollar" on my liquor cabinet. The coin went on to be used in the trial as government's exhibit B, even though I had never seen it before. Both the twenty-dollar bill and the gold-plated silver dollar were planted evidence.

The kicker, though, came when the FBI claimed a plastic water jug containing $98,600 had been discovered buried in my neighbor's, the Sinkles, yard on June 26, 1972. When I buried the money, there had been one hundred and twenty thousand dollars. That sum was reduced to $98,600. Where did the remaining $21,400 go? Into FBI pockets, I'm guessing, but it doesn't matter. Either way, that statement was a blatant lie. The FBI additionally claimed that the money was being processed as of June 26, 1972. Later, I found proof that the cash was in the FBI lab before May 27.

The search warrants for my home and my car were issued by two different federal magistrates but were based completely on a perjured search warrant affidavit. I told my attorney that I was certain the government was fabricating evidence and had searched the car illegally before June 2. Unfortunately, we had no way of proving that—at least not yet.

"Why do you think the FBI would do something like that?" Sherman asked.

"That's what they do," I responded. In every federal prosecution, an FBI agent is assigned as the case agent. My case agent was Special Agent Paul Chamberlin. Nothing I had done in my entire career as a safe cracker could measure up to the illegal tricks Chamberlin and his subordinate agents—including Special Agent Francis Calley, Special Agent James Conway, Special Agent Carol Pilkist, Special Agent James Cagnosola, and Special Agent Irvin B. Wells—pulled during the investigation and trial of my case.

I may have been a thief, but all the tricks that the federal government, from the FBI agents to the U.S. Attorneys to the federal judges, pulled to make a case were the real crime. Their "by any means necessary" attitude was pretty common knowledge at that time, and I was becoming more and more certain that the government was going to use all the underhanded tricks it could think of to convict me. I had been so careful that they needed to pull all the stops.

I was desperate to find out whether the fingerprint on the battery was a real latent print or if the FBI had manufactured it. I told my attorney to hire an expert fingerprint examiner. The expert said it was a real latent print, which meant it was not photographed onto the battery or affixed to the battery by some other means.

The more I realized how far the federal government was going to go to get me convicted, the angrier I became. There I was, sitting in jail, and I was certain that evidence was being planted against me. I wanted to do everything in my power to prove that the federal government was cheating, so I had my brother hire the American Bureau of Investigation, a private investigation firm based in Santa Ana, California, in the hope that a detective might be able to find out some information. I specifically wanted to know on what date the FBI actually searched the 1962 Oldsmobile. With that information, we could start to put together a case against them.

That turned out to be a good move, because the very next day, an investigator from the agency told my brother that he had found proof that the FBI had searched the car about two weeks before June 2. After they searched it, they towed the car to the Orange County Sheriff's Department. Hearing that news, I was certain that was the real reason the FBI didn't want Chuck near Earl's house on June 2. Just as I had suspected, the car was already gone. The feds did not want anyone to know that.

It felt good to finally have some corroboration of my suspicions, but my excitement was short-lived. When my brother called the agency to speak with the investigator several days later, he was told that the man had been transferred out of state and that the agency knew nothing about his ongoing investigations. When my brother gave me that excuse, I was certain the FBI had my brother's phone tapped. They had obviously listened in on his conversation with the detective and then confronted the investigator, warning him to keep his nose out of the case.

When I told my attorney what my brother had learned from the investigator, he immediately went to the Orange County Sheriff's Office. He talked to a detective there who said he didn't know anything about the FBI's investigation of the burglary or the search of the car. That was another lie. On the night the news of the robbery broke, I watched a television report stating that both the FBI and the Orange County Sheriff's Department were investigating the crime. There is no way the Sheriff's Office was unaware of the ongoing federal investigation. But it seemed obvious that the police department was too afraid to contradict anything the FBI said.

Our first real evidence that the FBI was lying didn't come until the pretrial. Unfortunately, neither my attorneys nor I realized just how explosive the information was until far too late. Things were happening very quickly, and in pretrial discovery, we started receiving FBI laboratory reports concerning examinations conducted on the tools and other items found during the search of the car and my home.

A laboratory report dated June 23, 1972, listed tools the FBI claimed had been found in the car search. This, remember, was the search they claimed was conducted on June 2. Each item had a "K" before it, beginning with "K-4" and going up to "K-84." There was also a separate list of items labeled beginning with "Q."

At the time of our trial, none of us knew what the letters "K" or "Q" meant on FBI laboratory reports. I figured it out only about a year after the trial. When an FBI agent sends an item to the laboratory for examination as potential evidence, the first thing the laboratory does is log the item, document the date on which it was received, and note which case it belongs to. The item is then sent to a laboratory examiner with specific expertise relating to the object. For example, tool marks, gun barrel rifling, latent fingerprints, and so forth.

The laboratory examiner gives the first received item in a case a "Q-1" label. "Q" stands for questionable evidence. The next item would receive a "Q-2" designation, and so on, until all of the evidence had been properly labeled. After the laboratory examiner has finished with an item, he switches it to a "K" label, which means the item has been examined and the results of the examination are known. For example, let's say "Q-1" was examined. After testing, the results of the examination would be revealed. The "Q-1" item would then become a "K-1" item, and the FBI laboratory examiner would create a report explaining the results of his examination on that item.

Looking back at the June 23 laboratory report, it shows all "K" lettered items being sent from Los Angeles to the FBI laboratory to be examined. During my trial, that laboratory report was the government's trial exhibit D, and during the trial, FBI agent Roger Goldsberry testified that on June 6, he sent the items listed on the report to the FBI laboratory in Washington, D.C. Two days later, on June 8, the laboratory received the items.

The "K" items. Not the "Q" files.

In other words, according to the FBI, on June 6, FBI agent Roger Goldsberry sent the laboratory all the "K" lettered items listed on the June 23 laboratory report. That meant he was actually sending items that had already been examined in the laboratory and assigned a "K" letter.

In fact, it was actually sometime between May 24 and June 2 when the FBI searched the car, meaning the search was illegally done without a warrant. Moreover, I have since become convinced that my neighbor's son did not see me bury the jug of money with one hundred and twenty thousand dollars in it while his mother had him sleeping on the porch. That was a fabrication. In reality, it was the FBI agents who were living in my neighbor's home that saw me bury the jug. No doubt they dug it up soon after I buried it. I also believe that soon after the FBI agents dug up the jug of money, they burglarized my garage. They did all of this while living in the Sinkles' home and spying on me. I know you must think it's amazing that law enforcement would go to such lengths to convict a person, but I've learned that government is far more corrupt than any crook I know. And I do know a lot of crooks. Just ask Richard Nixon.

To make matters worse, the FBI found the condo we had used as our base of operations in California. My brother and Chuck had been right to worry about its proximity to the bank, but the fact that the feds managed to locate it meant someone had talked. I knew the snitch wasn't my brother or Chuck. Those guys were solid. My money was on Phil or Broeckels.

When the police interviewed the owners of the condo, they couldn't identify any of us. They had only ever met Ronnie Barber. Sending someone unconnected to the robbery turned out to have been a really smart call.

But it wasn't enough to save us from the FBI's corruption.

An initial search of the condo produced no evidence that we had been there. We were very careful and hadn't even left a fingerprint behind. But the feds weren't going to let that pass. All of a sudden, one day, they claimed they had found plates in the dishwasher with fingerprints on them, fingerprints that were eventually identified as those of Amil Dinsio, James Dinsio, and Charles Mulligan. In the pictures of the evidence, the dishes are perfectly free of food smudges.

How do fingerprints stay on dishes that have already clearly been through a rinse cycle? They get planted, that's how. The FBI and the U.S. Attorney had to place each of us close to the score, and that's how they chose to do it.

While all this was going on, Earl Dawson and his wife testified that June 2 was the first time they met the FBI agents who came to their home to ask them about the car. They said the agents searched the car on that date, eventually finding the incriminating flashlight battery. I've already shown that this timeline was a lie, but Earl and his wife stood by their story.

The Dawsons went on to testify that in early March 1972, Chuck and I came to their house and met with both of them. They said that Chuck returned later and asked to store the car there. This meeting never took place. It is an outright lie.

Moreover, in a pretrial suppression hearing, Mrs. Dawson testified that she had allowed FBI Agent Roger Goldsberry to use her camera to take photographs of the car while it was sitting in her garage. On cross-examination, when she was asked what kind of a camera she owned, she testified it was a little camera in which the film had to be removed to be developed. She insisted that it was not a Polaroid camera. When Roger Goldsberry was asked why he used her camera rather than one issued by the FBI, he claimed that his supervisor had never ordered a camera.

In hindsight, I realize my attorneys didn't always do the best job on the case. They should have pressed the issue of Mrs. Dawson letting Goldsberry use her camera to take pictures. They should have hired a professional photographer to look at the photographs. Goldsberry and Mrs. Dawson would have been caught red-handed in their lie. Years later, my nephew went to the Clerk's office and obtained copies of the photos Goldsberry maintained that he took using Mrs. Dawson's "little" camera. The photographs, the government's exhibits 112-A through 112-G (see photos of some of the exhibits on pages 166-167), were clearly taken with a Polaroid camera, a Polaroid camera with a wide-angle lens hefty enough to encompass the car's extended trunk.

That type of camera is the exact one standardly issued to FBI agents.

Agent Goldsberry testified that all the items in the car's trunk were photographed just as they were found. Anyone looking at the photographs can clearly see that the items had been moved and tampered with. For example, the photographs marked 112-D and 112-E show a white paper bag with a tear in it. In those two pictures, the bag is lying in the same position in the car's trunk. But the white paper bag in picture 112-F has been moved. Even crazier, the bag is not the same bag. The tear is a completely different shape and size than the tear in pictures 112-D and 112-E.

The trial unfolded in a similar fashion. One FBI agent after another sauntered into the court and swore that the initial search of the Oldsmobile took place on June 2. FBI lab examiners testified under oath about when the tools were first examined in the FBI's laboratory.

I was watching them perjure right in front of my face and there was nothing I could do to stop them.

The trial judge was William M. Byrne. To this day, I am certain he was aware of the underhanded maneuverings of the prosecution. But he was a biased judge, and a biased judge always goes out of his way to cover up for government misconduct.

The judge's collaboration can easily be explained. The United States Department of Justice, which was in charge of prosecuting my case, is the branch that gives the final okay to a person recommended for a federal judgeship. In order to receive a federal judgeship, the candidate must submit to an FBI investigation. If the candidate is found to be honest and in good legal standing, the United States Justice Department recommends the person to Congress. Congress then holds hearings on the issue. Finally, the President of the United States has the option to accept or deny the appointment. So the Department of Justice was responsible for giving Judge Byrne his position. Of course they found someone who would be on their side.

The judge denied all the suppression motions my attorneys filed against the federal search warrants.

In 1972, the United States Attorney in Los Angeles was William Keller. Along with his assistant, Jack Walters, Keller acted in collusion with their witnesses, convincing those such as Mrs. Dawson to lie during testimony. Mr. Keller was given a federal judgeship on October 4, 1982. Mr. Walters was handed the same boon on June 7, 2002. Their hard work paid off.

The bottom line is that the whole federal court system is prejudicially stacked against any defendant who might run afoul of the FBI or the Department of Justice. I was a defendant like that. A federal judgeship is a lifetime job, and for a person to get that job, he or she has to continue to play ball with the United States Department of Justice for as long as they want to keep their job. That means conspiring with FBI agents and innocent citizens to prepare them for perjuries and to fabricate and plant evidence. If you are an honest U.S. Attorney, if you don't go along with the FBI agents in fabricating and planting evidence and in preparing suborned perjuries for your trial witnesses, you will never become a United States District Court Judge. My case is evidence of that sad fact.

Since the Department of Justice has control over whether a Federal District Court judge gets and keeps a judgeship, the Department of Justice has control over judges in any given trial. This prejudice comes into play at key moments, like when the judge is making a decision on suppressing evidence or on other important rulings in a trial. Once a person becomes a United States District Court Judge, he becomes a "puppet" for the "puppeteer."

Another important piece of information is that in early 1972, the FBI's director, J. Edgar Hoover, died. President Nixon was looking for a new FBI Director to take his place. So in 1972, at the very time of our trial, President Nixon sent his right hand man in the White House, John D. Ehrlichman, to see our trial judge, Matthew Byrne, and offer him a job as the FBI's director. Judge Byrne declined the offer, but I've always wondered whether that was really the reason the President sent his right hand man to see Judge Byrne. The alternative possibility is that Tricky Dick was just making sure Judge Byrne denied all our suppression motions and made sure we all got convicted for stealing his extorted millions. This theory was commonly believed during the trial. I thought we should move for a mistrial.

At the end of the trial, I was convicted and sentenced to twenty years in prison. I almost couldn't believe the news. I just sat there, in a cold sweat, and accepted my fate, while the judge, the FBI agents, and all the others who perjured themselves at my trial, got away scot free.

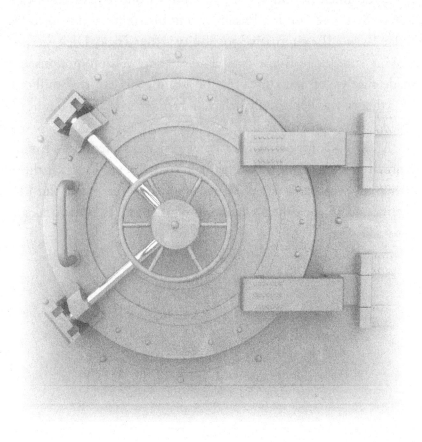

Chapter Thirteen

The Lordstown Trial

While I was waiting in the Los Angeles County Jail to be transferred to a federal penitentiary, I was indicted for the Lordstown Bank burglary on top of the other charges. I couldn't believe they were on to me on that score, too. The only thought that entered my mind was, "What are those dirty feds up to now? What evidence could they possibly have to convict me for *that* job?" My brother, Chuck, and I had been meticulous.

I knew the United States Department of Justice could indict a hamburger, with or without condiments, if they wanted to, but I was no hamburger. My brother and Chuck would never rat me out. I knew that better than I knew anything, so I didn't admit to anything yet. I figured I'd just wait and see what the government had against me when we got to trial in Cleveland.

I was in the Cuyahoga County Jail for over a year waiting to stand trial for the Lordstown Bank burglary. While I was there, the Watergate trial was all over the news. Even those of us who were locked up managed to catch some of it on television.

It seemed to me that Nixon went wrong hiring an amateur crew of burglars with G. Gordon Liddy at their head. If my boys had done it, we wouldn't have been stupid enough to get caught on a simple job like the Watergate complex.

Jail is no vacation. Living with hundreds of cockroaches and mice running in and out of holes in the walls makes it even worse. While I awaited my second trial, I killed time playing poker and buying the guys tons of smokes and candy bars. I was liked, or at least I thought I was. But one day, one of the guys left for court and didn't come back until the late afternoon. I didn't think anything about it; people were in and out for court dates all the time. But the next morning, he came to my cell and told me that he hadn't gone to court at all. The truth was much scarier.

He told me that when he left the jail the day before, he was brought before two men who said they were FBI agents. One of the men told my fellow prisoner that he was a suspect in the bombing of a phone company and that they wanted to discuss it with him.

"Man, was I scared," the prisoner said. "I told them I didn't know shit about any bombing." But the FBI agents insisted on taking him to their office anyway. Once there, they were very polite. They even gave him a soda, a rare treat in jail. They admitted that they knew he didn't have anything to do with any bombing. They just wanted to talk.

That was when one of the agents asked if he knew Amil Dinsio.

When the prisoner told me that, my blood ran cold. My buddy had been too terrified to remember the agents' names, but that didn't matter in the end. The agents asked if he would like to go home to his wife and have the charges brought against him dropped. He said he would love that. In good time, the agents revealed the string attached to the deal. From my perspective, it was a big one.

"You can go home today if you agree to testify that Amil Dinsio told you he burglarized a bank in Warren, Ohio." The agents had the wrong information about the bank's location. The bank burglarized was the Second National Bank of Warren's *Lordstown*

Branch. The agents didn't even have the facts straight and they were still determined to prosecute me.

My fellow prisoner was a good guy, and I still am grateful to him for standing his ground. He refused to lie just to save his own skin. The agents accepted his decision but warned him not to say anything to me about the conversation. They threatened him that if they heard he had, they would make sure he would never get probation.

I called my Cleveland attorney, Milton Schulman, and updated him on what I had learned. He wanted to alert the judge, but I told him that I didn't want to hurt my buddy's chances of getting probation. The FBI agents would know immediately who had let the information slip, unless they had approached other prisoners, too, which wouldn't surprise me, but it wasn't worth the risk. In the end, all Milton did was get a sworn statement from the prisoner in case we needed it down the road.

The entire incident assured me that the FBI didn't have much evidence against me in the Lordstown case. If they had a stable case, they wouldn't resort to the same pathetic, underhanded tactics they had pulled in California.

After that little incident, it was just a waiting game until the government gave us more discovery material on the evidence it was intending to use at trial. I was confident they didn't have anything. Even my attorney said he didn't see how they could even take the case to trial.

I should have known better.

Sometime after the FBI tried to convince my fellow prisoner to lie, I received a visit from both of my attorneys. Milton and his son, Jack, asked me if I'd had a pickup truck sitting in my yard when the Lordstown bank was burglarized. I didn't own a pickup truck, but I thought carefully about the time of the burglary. The only old truck that was ever sitting in my yard belonged to 4-Wheels Auto Sales.

I sometimes used it to haul trash and debris to a nearby strip-mine dump. I asked Milton and Jack why they wanted to know.

Milton told me that FBI agents were claiming they had found a truck tire track in the dirt driveway by the bank. They had made a cast of it and were now saying it matched one of the tires on the truck that had been sitting in my yard. The U.S. Attorney Tim Potts and the FBI agents were hatching a plan to prove I had used the truck to haul the money from the bank. To this day, I still remember my exact words to Milton and Jack.

"Those idiots are nuts. Why would I need a truck to haul away four hundred and thirty thousand dollars, unless the money was in pennies and dimes? The only thing I ever hauled in that truck was trash. The headlights and taillights don't even work. It's not even safe to take out at night, unless you're a fool."

My attorneys informed me that the FBI had obtained a search warrant, gone to 4-Wheels, and took the tires off the truck in order to send them to the FBI's laboratory.

"Are you sure the lights don't work?" Milton asked.

"Hell yeah, I'm sure," I said. "That thing is a piece of shit. Anyone would be nuts to drive that heap at night. And doing anything more than fifty makes the front end shimmy. If I wanted to haul loot away from a score, that truck would be the last vehicle I would choose."

Both attorneys just sat there gaping. They couldn't believe how far the FBI would go to fabricate evidence. The more I thought about it, the more certain I was that the FBI agents who had been watching my house before the warrants were issued must have snuck across the street onto my property sometime after dark and made a plaster cast from the truck tire. How else could the FBI have found that tire print? The Lordstown Bank is a good twenty-five miles from my home, and the truck never went near it. I told my lawyers to go to 4-Wheels and talk to the machinist. He could verify the truck had no working headlights and was not road-worthy, especially after dark.

Jack Schulman looked the truck over and got a statement from the owner of 4-Wheels and the mechanic confirming the truck's poor condition. Not long after that, we had a hearing to request the suppression of the tire track casting and the truck tire as evidence. I told my attorney that I wanted to see the cast of the tire print and the FBI laboratory report, as well as the pictures matching the tire to the cast. Sure enough, the laboratory report showed the cast matched the tire. The picture of the casting had little arrows pointing to the similarities to the picture of the tire. I couldn't believe what a bunch of framing bastards those agents were.

After we put forward evidence that the truck had no working headlights and that the light's wiring under the dashboard had been burned up for years, the U.S. Attorney changed his tune, claiming to the court that the tire casting and the truck tire were not an exact match after all.

When the judge heard that, there was nothing he could do, no matter how biased he was. The tire track was tossed out. You can bet if the judge had allowed the tire as evidence, an FBI agent would have been right up there testifying the tire was a perfect match to the cast.

While we were arguing to suppress the plaster cast, we were also having a suppression hearing to stop the government from using the $98,600 and two small pieces of paper as evidence. The FBI claimed that the first piece of paper, a scrap with figures written on it, was found with the money in the jug. They claimed it matched the second piece of paper, which the FBI said they found in my home on June 27, 1972, during their search. Those two pieces of paper connected me to the money.

Next, the U.S. Attorney told the court that when the FBI searched my garage on June 27, they found a jug matching the one

I had used to bury the one hundred and twenty thousand dollars. Both jugs were sitting on a table in front of the judge. They looked identical. I have always wondered where the FBI bought that second jug, because they sure as hell didn't find it in my garage. The government's whole purpose was to tie me to the money through the jugs and the paper just like they tied me to the 1962 Oldsmobile using the flashlight battery and my fingerprints.

The rest of the prosecution's case was full of more lies. For example, the U.S. Attorney told the court that the FBI had identified one of the one-hundred-dollar bills from the money in the jug as one that was shipped from the Federal Reserve Bank in Cleveland, Ohio, to the Second National Bank of Warren's main bank in downtown Warren. He told the court that on the day of the burglary, a Brink's armored truck picked up a shipment of money from the Second National Bank in downtown Warren and delivered it to their branch bank in Lordstown, clearly implying that the one-hundred-dollar bill that was shipped from the Federal Reserve to the Second National Bank in Warren was stolen in the burglary and then found among the $98,600.

There was not a thread of evidence to support that claim, especially given the fact that the FBI had arrested Goldstein for exchanging Lordstown money in banks in Canton. How could that bill have made it into the jug?

Unfortunately, the court denied the motions to suppress the two jugs, the $98,600, the one-hundred-dollar bill, and the bits of paper. We may have won the battle of the tire casting, but we lost the war. The majority of the fabricated evidence was allowed to go through.

While I was in jail awaiting trial, Jack Schulman came to visit with the offer of a deal. He had just spoken with the U.S. Attorney. He had been informed that if I would plead guilty to the Lordstown burglary, the government would consent to a ten-year sentence running concurrently with the twenty-year sentence I had received in California. I didn't even have to think about it.

"Hell no," I said. "I'm not about to plead guilty. That's exactly what they want." At the time, I was hoping to get a reversal in California. I didn't want to be stuck in prison on a ten-year sentence I had agreed to just to get a plea bargain. I also figured I would beat the Lordstown case. It didn't seem like they had any evidence against me.

Several days before the trial, Jack and Milton told me that the government had a witness. The witness was Charley Broeckels.

"He claims he did the Lordstown job with you," Milton told me.

"You're kidding me." I was so stunned that I could barely react.

My lawyer handed me Charley's statement.

"He wasn't on the score," I insisted. "What the hell is he doing?" I read the statement. Sure enough, Charley was claiming to have been on that burglary with my brother and me. He didn't mention Chuck. Right then, I knew Broeckels was the one who gave the FBI the information about the condo and all the rest of the Laguna Niguel job. No wonder the FBI found the car and condo. That asshole had put the finger right on us, and now the FBI was telling him exactly what to say about Lordstown.

I knew the FBI must have had something on Broeckels in order to force him to talk about the California job. I told my lawyers as much. In all likelihood, they were putting the pressure on him for one of his past murders. I called Butchie and demanded he come to the jail right away. Once he arrived, looking sweaty and nervous, I told him that Broeckels was going to testify against me.

"He fucking claims he was in on the Lordstown bank burglary."

"No way." Butchie was as surprised as I was. "That's completely insane." Butchie promised me he'd go talk with Broeckels. But when Butchie visited the next day, he said Broeckels wasn't anywhere to be found. Even his girlfriend claimed she didn't know where he was. Butchie thought she was lying.

"I should have killed him a long time ago," Butchie said. He was so mad I thought he might kill the next person he saw.

There was nothing we could do. I learned later that Broeckels and his girlfriend had already been put in the Federal Witness Program. He made a deal with the government. They would forget about his murder charge in exchange for help convicting me for Lordstown.

The trial for the Lordstown burglary finally commenced. The waiting was over. The court heard testimony from the bank manager who had told the deputies that if the bell wasn't ringing, there was nothing to worry about, and that he'd have the alarm fixed in the morning. My neighbor, Natalie Sinkle, and her son, Michael, also spoke. Michael testified that on June 26, 1972, he was mowing the lawn and spotted something sticking out of the ground. When he investigated, he found the jug.

This was an outright contradiction to his story during my bail bond hearing, when he claimed he had been sleeping on the front porch and had seen me bury the jug. This was yet another sign that the FBI was running the show. Clearly, the agents and the prosecuting attorney realized they had to change their story when they finally figured out that they had forgotten one key fact.

The Sinkle's house didn't have a front porch.

When I purchased the transcript of the bond hearing, the section concerning the neighbor boy was missing.

I knew that the United States Attorney and the FBI agents conspired with fourteen-year-old Michael Sinkle and his mother to contrive a perjured trial testimony. Your government forcing a fourteen-year-old kid to commit perjury—pretty hard to swallow. I figure the government paid them over twenty thousand dollars for their perjuries, the money missing from the jug. How low could the Department of Justice go?

The government then called in Agent Clyde Merryman to testify. Merryman claimed that he went to the Sinkle home on June 26, 1972, and took possession of the jug of money. After he got back to the FBI office, he found there to be $98,600 all in fifty-dollar and hundred-dollar bills. When asked in cross-examination if there were any bills bigger than that, he answered no. No mention was made of the five-hundred- and one-thousand-dollar bills I had placed in the jug.

At one point in his testimony, Merryman "slipped" on a question. He said, "When I found, I mean, when I was given the money."

This wasn't the first mistake the FBI had made in the trial, and it wouldn't be the last. No one seemed willing to point out the error. I was seething in my chair. The slip was just further proof that Michael Sinkle never found the money. My guess is that Agent Merryman was camped out spying from the Sinkle home. He probably saw me bury the jug in May of 1972, long before the illegal search warrant was issued.

The government then called Charley Broeckels to testify. They brought him out of protection to make an appearance. While under oath, he claimed that he was on the Lordstown bank burglary with me, my brother, and Chuck, though he only stood watch and never went into the bank.

The government next produced Federal Reserve Bank records that showed that eighteen million dollars, all in one-hundred-dollar bills, was withdrawn from one of the vaults in the Federal Reserve Bank in Cleveland, Ohio, and taken via a Brink's armored truck to the Second National Bank of Warren, Ohio. An employee from the Federal Reserve Bank testified that, according to its serial number, the one-hundred-dollar bill was one of the bills that was withdrawn from the Federal Reserve Bank vault and sent to the Second National Bank in Warren, Ohio.

The United States Attorney stood before the trial jury waving that one-hundred-dollar bill. He said the bill had been found in the buried jug. It was circumstantial evidence and never should have been permitted in court. Of course, the judge allowed it to stand.

As I sat in the courtroom, Tim Potts stacked the $98,600 on a table in front of the jurors. I could see the members of the jury staring at that cash, the wheels in their heads turning. I knew then and there that I was going to be convicted. After all, in 1974, that was big time money. I knew what the jurors were thinking. They couldn't imagine where I would have come up with that kind of cash without stealing it. I have to admit, that would have been tricky.

I was convicted of the Lordstown bank burglary and sentenced to ten years in prison, consecutive to the twenty-year sentence I had received in California. United States Marshals transported me to the federal penitentiary in Leavenworth, Kansas. I did eight years before being paroled on October 5, 1980.

In 1974, while I was in prison, the United States Freedom of Information Act, 5 U.S.C. 522(a), was rewritten to make it easy for anyone to get government records from government agencies. I filed a request with the United States Department of Justice in Washington, D.C., for the records the FBI compiled on me.

In 1975, acting FBI Director Patrick Gray, Tricky Dick's man, was replaced by FBI Director Clarence M. Kelly. Kelly was appointed by President Gerald Ford. In a letter to me dated November 7, 1975, Director Kelly informed me that seventy-nine pages of FBI documents on me had been located. I sent the required processing fee. The records were promptly forwarded over. A month later, Director Kelly wrote again to tell me that an additional ninety-three pages had been located. I sent another small processing fee and received those documents as well.

I didn't hear from the government for some time. Then, in 1976, I was notified that a large number of FBI records pertaining to my case had been found. Again, I sent a processing fee. This time I was mailed three giant boxes.

The paperwork included photographs, letters, agents' investigation reports, laboratory results, and numerous other FBI documents that I had never seen. Most had been heavily redacted, but I could read between the lines.

As I was looking through the hundreds of documents, I found an FBI memorandum dated June 27, 1972, that showed that $98,600 had been sent to the FBI's lab. The "by subject" line had been redacted, obviously to hide Sidney Goldstein's name, since at the time of the FBI laboratory report, Sidney Goldstein had not even been arrested. The June 27, 1972, date on the FBI memorandum was a false date.

When the FBI arrests someone, that person's fingerprints are immediately sent to the FBI's headquarters in D.C. There, they are filed under that person's name. Forever more, they will show up in a search whenever that person is investigated. Looking back at the July 12 latent fingerprint report on page two, it clearly stated that no fingerprint record was located for Sidney Goldstein. I wondered why not.

If Sidney Goldstein was arrested on May 27, 1972, then why weren't his fingerprints already in the files on July 12? This clearly points to the fact that the $98,600 was in the FBI's laboratory before he was arrested. It also means that the FBI's July 12 laboratory report is falsely dated.

It also means that during my Lordstown bank burglary trial, the United States Attorney suborned perjuries from the government's trial witnesses, Natalie Sinkle, and her son, Michael, on finding the $98,600 on June 26.

That discovery, however, was only the tip of the iceberg. As

DATE:

ATTENTION EXPEDITE

TO: ACTING DIRECTOR, F.B.I.
(Attention: F.B.I. Laboratory)

FROM: SAC, LOS ANGELES

SUBJECT: UNSUB(S)
UNITED CALIFORNIA BANK
Laguna Niguel Office
6 Monarch Bay Plaza
Laguna Niguel, California, 3/24/72 BB

Being forwarded under separate cover are the following items:

1. Three (3) rolls black tape.

2. Seven (7) gloves: four (4) right hand, three (3) left hand.

3. Two (2) chisels.

4. Eleven (11) flashlight batteries.

5. Three (3) torch cutting tips.

6. Four (4) test-lead wires.

7. Two (2) transceiver carrying cases.

The above items were obtained from subject, Amil Alfred Dinsio's (F.B.I. #204237E) detached garage at his residence.

1. The laboratory is requested to compare the tapes submitted in the above captioned case with the tapes in #1.

2. Mineralogical examination requested on item #2 to determine if any cement particles are present to compare with cement submitted in the above captioned case.

3. Toolmark examinations requested on item #3 to determine if they can be associated with toolmark on safe deposit box doors in the above captioned case.

4. The latent fingerprint section, identification division, is requested to process items in #4 and 7 for latent print. After processing, the identification division should compare any latent prints developed with those of subject Dinsio mentioned above and 24 others mentioned in letter dated 5/22/72.

5. Compare item in #5 to determine if the torch cutting tips will attached to either of the cutting torches submitted from the search of the 1962 Oldsmobile in the above captioned case.

6. The test-lead wires in item #6 should be examined to determine if they will plug into the Triplett volt-ohm milliammeter recovered in the search of the 1962 Oldsmobile in the above captioned case.

7. After latent examination on items in #7 they should be examined to determine if the transceivers obtained in the search of the 1962 Oldsmobile will fit into the carrying cases.

After examinations, all items should be returned to Los Angeles. Any latents should be retained and the results forwarded.

I continued looking through the FBI documents, I found the "prince" of all evidence. That was an undated FBI document with the words "ATTENTION EXPEDITE" underlined. The document was sent to the FBI's acting director with the subject, "UNSUB(S) UNITED CALIFORNIA BANK, Laguna Niguel Office, 6 Monarch Bay Plaza, Laguna Niguel, California, 3/24/72 BB." (See page 144.)

This undated FBI document shows that FBI agents burglarized my garage for the sole purpose of finding an item with my fingerprints on it. Number 4 on the top half of the document clearly shows that FBI agents stole eleven flashlight batteries along with the other listed items in Numbers 1, 2, 3, 5, 6, and 7 on the top half. After Number 7, it states this: "The above items were obtained from subject, Amil Alfred Dinsio's (F.B.I. # 204237E) detached garage at his residence."

On the bottom half of the document, at Number 4, the FBI agent who submitted the stolen items asked the FBI's latent fingerprint division to look for my fingerprints on the items submitted in Numbers 4 and 7 above and on twenty-four other items mentioned in a letter dated May 22, 1972. At Numbers 5, 6, and 7, the document refers to the search of the 1962 Oldsmobile. Obviously, this is proof that at the time the FBI agents burglarized my garage, the FBI had already searched the Oldsmobile in California. The tools from the search were already in the FBI lab and had been examined.

Not only did the FBI agents steal my fingerprints to plant as evidence, but on June 27, 1972, an FBI agent and a United States Attorney in Cleveland, Ohio, prepared a bogus affidavit in support of a bogus search warrant for my home. In the affidavit, the government used the stolen flashlight battery from my garage as probable cause in front of a United States Magistrate to issue the search warrant, claiming the battery was located in a flashlight during the search of the 1962 Oldsmobile.

In 1994, I filed a complaint with the then United States Attorney General, Janet Reno, asking her to investigate my allegation that FBI agents burglarized my garage. She referred my complaint to the FBI's Office of Professional Responsibility (OPR/DOJ). Basically, the Attorney General asked the Department of Justice to investigate itself.

Not much chance of that happening.

I eventually received a letter from William D. Gore in the Department of Justice. He told me that the OPR/FBI had conducted an inquiry of my complaint to the Attorney General and found no basis to substantiate my allegations. The letter claimed that a hearing had been held in 1977 in Akron, Ohio, concerning the same allegations, and that the court determined that I was unprepared and unjustified in my arguments.

But the hearing in Akron was not about FBI agents burglarizing my garage but in regards to my filing a 28 U.S.C. §2255 habeas corpus for my constitutional rights being violated during the Lordstown bank burglary trial. My 1994 complaint was closed. By that point, I wasn't exactly surprised.

I admit to committing the burglaries in Laguna Niguel and Lordstown. I don't think there's any doubt of that at this point in my story. But as I have mentioned in previous chapters, the crimes the government perpetrated in its pursuit of me were far worse than my own. I stole some cash. The FBI agents and U.S. Attorneys betrayed the trust of their offices by stooping to underhanded corruption and illegal acts.

In the first section of this book, I asked who the bigger crook was—thieves like me or the lying federal agents who go to any means necessary to get a conviction. I'm not sure I have the definitive answer to that one, though I certainly have an opinion. It's interesting to consider who does the most damage with their crimes. I was guilty of cracking some vaults. Through incredibly unfair means, I served my time.

But what happens when the FBI and the Justice Department go after some poor schmuck who just happened to be in the wrong place at the wrong time and has never committed any crime greater than jaywalking? Don't tell me it never happens. How is the average citizen meant to have any confidence in a government run by presidents who are little better than mafia men asking for protection money and policed by organizations willing to lie, cheat, and fabricate evidence to get the verdict they want?

Yes, I'm a thief. I'm a damn good one. But I only go after your money.

The U.S. government will take everything else.

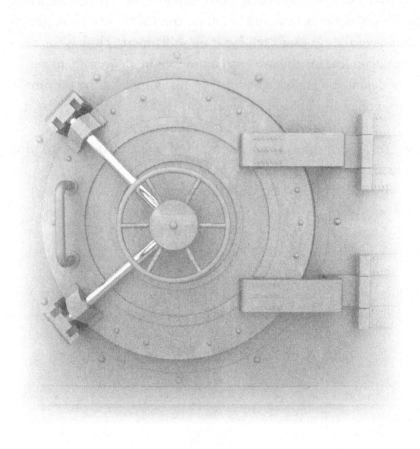

Epilogue

Once a Thief, Always a Thief

Forty years later, the underhanded workings of the federal government on my case still infuriate me. Many of the major players in the drama have moved on or passed away, leaving only me to tell the true story of what happened.

Pat Ferruccio

In the early 1990s, I learned that Ferruccio had been an FBI snitch for years. That explains why his right hand man, Sidney Goldstein, never went to prison for exchanging the Lordstown bank burglary money. To this day, I'm amazed I wasn't caught sooner or even killed in an FBI shootout. I suppose the only reason I made it out alive was simply because Ferruccio never knew which bank I was going to burglarize.

Jimmy Hoffa

Union leader Jimmy Hoffa continued to support Richard Nixon, even though he orchestrated the theft of the President's money in California. He disappeared in 1975, probably murdered on orders from the Italian mafia. To this day, no one has found his body. Some say it's buried in the New Jersey Meadowlands.

I've often wondered if Nixon ever found out that Hoffa was responsible for his millions going missing. Either way, Hoffa was declared dead in 1982.

President Richard Milhous Nixon

As most people know, Nixon was forced to resign in 1974 during the fallout from the Watergate scandal. I was sitting in the county jail in Cleveland, Ohio, waiting to go to trial for the Lordstown bank burglary when he left office. Surrounded by other criminals, I watched him give his resignation speech on the news.

In 2004, about thirty years after the Laguna bank score, I learned that three months after the burglary, the Teamsters Union, led by its president, Jimmy Hoffa, endorsed President Richard Nixon for re-election.

Phil Christopher

Butchie's cousin was convicted along with me and Chuck and received twenty years in prison. In December of 1976, while Phil was doing time in Terre Haute, Indiana, the FBI tried to make a deal with him. They would have Phil paroled if he would meet with my wife and try to find out where the loot from the Laguna bank burglary was hidden. He agreed and the parole went through.

But Pat Ferruccio got wind of what Phil was up to and warned Linda.

On January 16, 1977, about two weeks after Phil was paroled, a *Cleveland Plain Dealer* reporter, Mary Jane Woge, wrote an article focusing on why Phil, a convicted criminal, had received a parole so soon. The exposé brought a lot of attention to Phil's situation, so the FBI had the Parole Board rescind it, claiming a mistake had been made. In no time at all, the United States Marshals were hauling Phil back to prison. About two years later, Phil was paroled once again. That time it stuck.

In 1991, for no apparent reason, Phil signed statements with the Cuyahoga County prosecutors in Cleveland, Ohio, implicating two brothers from Cleveland in the pimp Prunella's murder. Twelve years later, while he was in federal prison serving time for selling drugs, he testified before a grand jury, getting the two brothers indicted for Prunella's murder.

In 2005, an author named Rick Porrello saw an opportunity to cash in on my reputation as a professional bank burglar. With all the publicity the news media and the FBI had generated about the Laguna Niguel bank burglary, Porrello teamed up with Phil to write a book titled *Super Thief*.

It's laughable that a petty criminal considers himself a "super thief."

In the book, Porrello has Phil in California beating the bank's alarm system and helping me drill holes in the concrete bank vault. Until the writing of this book, I have never told anyone how my brother and I drilled and blasted holes into bank vaults. That includes Phil. Porrello also had Phil on the Lordstown bank burglary, just like the FBI put Broeckels on the job. That, of course, is another lie. All in all, it was a good story by Mr. Porrello. Too bad not a word of it was true.

Today, Phil lives in Cleveland. He is doing federal-supervised release for selling drugs. He gave up being a "Super Thief" and went into peddling dope. That is a definite downgrade in the criminal world.

Once a rat, always a rat.

James Dinsio and Ronnie Barber

My brother and Ronnie were both found not guilty of bank burglary but were sentenced to fifteen years apiece on charges of bank larceny and conspiracy. Each man spent six years in prison. Ronnie Barber died in the 1990s due to the effects of Agent Orange. My brother died of cancer in 2008 at the age of seventy-eight.

Harry "Ace" Barber

Harry went into hiding for eight years. He was living in Brookville, Pennsylvania, a small town just off of Interstate 80, when he was finally arrested on May 12, 1979. Although the FBI will never admit it, they had known where Harry was for years. They just didn't want to go through another trial. As a result, Harry was left alone until I was about to come up for parole in 1980. Knowing that I had documented evidence of their wrongdoing, the FBI arrested and tried Harry before I could get free to advise his legal counsel.

Harry did three years in prison. Now he lives in California, taking care of his mother.

Charles "Chuck" Mulligan

Chuck was sentenced to twenty years in prison for his part in the bank burglary. After serving his time, he retired and went to live in Ohio. He said that he felt guilty about Earl Dawson's role in betraying us—since Earl was Chuck's friend. I refuse to leave any of the blame with Chuck. Earl was a rat, just like Phil. Nothing will ever change that. Chuck passed away in 2014.

Charley Broeckels

Broeckels was never indicted on bank burglary in California, a sure sign that he was the FBI's informant. He was placed in the Witness Protection Program, as were Earl Dawson and his wife.

Broeckels was eventually moved to a town in Tennessee and given a new identity. While there, he burglarized a schoolteacher's home and was arrested.

The FBI had the charges dropped.

In the 1980s, Broeckels went before a county grand jury in Cleveland, Ohio, and testified that Phil Christopher was responsible for the murder of Dr. Price, the man killed during Broeckels and Phil's robbery of his home. One rat turning on another.

Broeckels has since died of rectal cancer.

Amil Dinsio

My wife Linda, my daughters, Melissa and Amie-Jo, and my two granddaughters have stood by my side through everything.

For years in the 1960s and 1970s, my crew and I had a monopoly on bank burglaries. We were known as some of the best professionals in the business. I often think about those days with pride. My crowning glory was the Laguna Niguel bank vault burglary. My good work there was only undone because of the government's deceitful methods of prosecution.

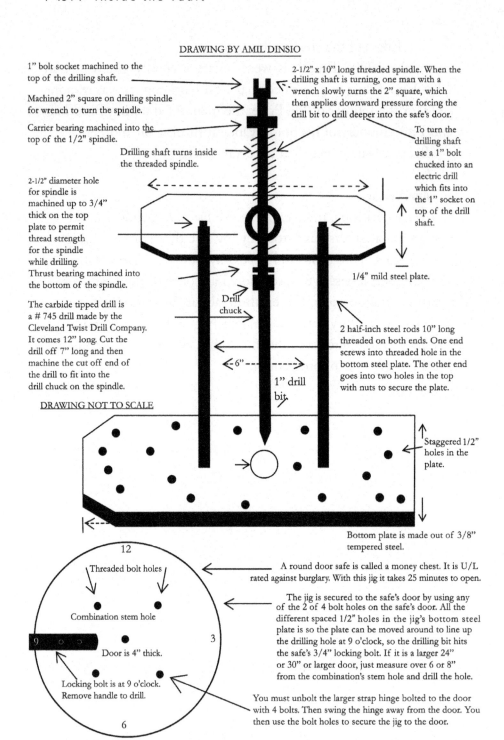

Epilogue: Once a Thief, Always a Thief / 155 /

DRAWING BY AMIL DINSIO

This illustration describes how to bypass a bank's alarm system using a pulser alarm. That means it is an electrical current or voltage whose value is normally a constant beating per second of pulses.

This pulser alarm is sending 10 to 18 pulses per second over (2) telephone line wires, traveling from a bank to a police station where there is an alarm pulser receiving module. If the pulses stop, the receiving module beeps and alerts the police. The (2) phone wires have (5) to (8) volts direct current (+) (-) flowing over them.

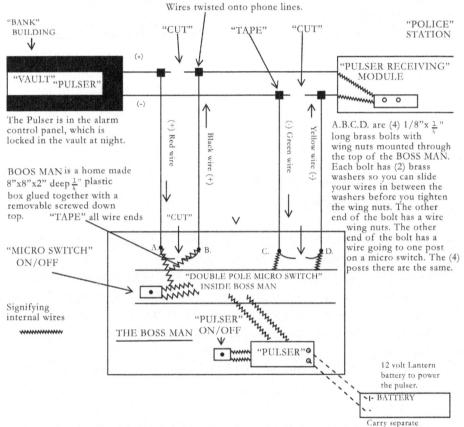

***Very important. Always remember to make the (4) "CUTS" as shown above. If those "CUTS" are not made you can't bypass the alarm system.

Also remember, before you attempt to best any alarm system, you must read the phone lines to find out if you can beat it. After you find out what alarm the bank has, build a bypass box to beat it.

BYPASSING A BANK'S ALARM

First, if a bank setting is in a good location and it is possible for you to find the (2) telephone line wires carrying the bank's alarm, you want to bypass the alarm system from outside the bank instead of going into the bank...just in case you accidently set off the alarm while you are attempting to bypass it. Safety to get away always comes first.

To do that you buy a spool of (20) or (22) gauge stranded copper (4) conductor electric cable for as many feet long as you need to do the job, to get you to a safe place in bushes or some other safe place where you will be when you are tying into the alarm. Inside the spool of cable are (4) colored plastic coated copper wires. Lets say the colors are red, black, green and yellow as used in the illustration. With those (4) different colored wires, you need to make (2) long wire loops. The length of the loops you determine by knowing how far away from the bank you need to get to be safe while you are bypassing the alarm.

Let's say you need to be 300 feet away from the bank. So you would buy a 300 foot long spool of cable. Now you unwind the cable off of the spool to get to the ends of the cable. After you find the ends...skin all (4) wires back about an inch to where you can see the copper. Then twist the red and black wires together real tight and tape it with black electrical tape. Then twist the green and yellow wires together and tape them the same way. Now you have (2) 300 foot long loops you need to beat the alarm. Then wind the cable back up on the spool leaving the (4) untaped ends showing so you can tie them onto telephone lines carrying the bank's alarm.

Now from your preliminary scouting of the bank, you should already have already located the (2) alarm wires which could be up a pole, on the back wall of the bank or in a telephone junction box on the ground.

When you are ready to do the job. Unwind your spool of cable and stretch it out until you have the (4) ends of your (2) loops at where you are going to tie into the telephone lines coming out of the bank carrying the alarm. Make sure you know which line is

(+) and which line is (−). Using a cigarette lighter to soften up the plastic coating on the telephone wires carrying the alarm...skin one wires at a time about an inch long in two places (3) or (4) inches apart from each other making sure the copper is showing and clean.

Then take either the red or the black and twist it around one of the skined telephone wires and tape it. Do the same with the other. Then **"CUT"** the telephone wire in between the (2) skinned places and tape those ends. Now do the same with the other green and yellow wires hooking them to the other telephone line. Now you have (2) 300 foot loops tied into the bank's alarm...extended away from the bank 300 feet away. You must remember which color of your (4) wires...the (2) that are heading to the police station...going from the bank...as the illustration shows.

On the illustration you see **BANK** and **POLICE**. Running between the bank and police are the (2) telephone line wires and you can see **"PULSER"** (it creates the alarm signal) heading to the police.

The best way to find the **PULSER** signal going over the telephone wires is by using an amplifier and it will let you hear the pulser beating. Then use your meter to determine which wire is (+) and which is (−).

Just follow the illustration when hooking to the **"BOSS MAN'S" A.B.C.D.** posts. The illustration shows that red and black is the (+) wire and green and yellow is the (−) wire. **NOTICE** the flow of the current. The black and yellow wires are heading to the police station. You must always know which color of your wires are heading to the police station.

As shown in the illustration. As soon as you have hooked onto the BOSS **MAN'S A,B.C.D.** posts and made the (4) **"CUTS"** the bank's alarm is flowing through one side of the micro switch and heading to the police. Then when you turn on your "PULSER" and and flip the micro switch...the bank's **PULSER** is stopped at the micro switch and your **"PULSER"** is now sending the alarm signal to the police. Now it is safe for you to go into the bank and get the money. When you are done and have all the loot away from the bank...just cut your (2) loops off the **BOSS MAN** and go home and count your **$$$$$$**.

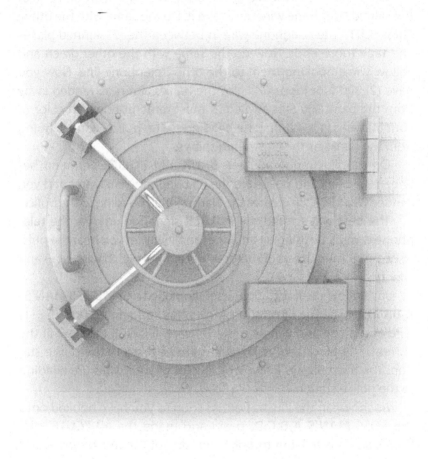

Photographs

Amil & his Brother James

Amil Dinsio

Amil, his wife Linda and two daughters, Melissa and Amie-Jo in Leavenworth

/ 160 / Photographs

Amil Dinsio with vault

Lordstown Bank

Ladder going up to alarm bell

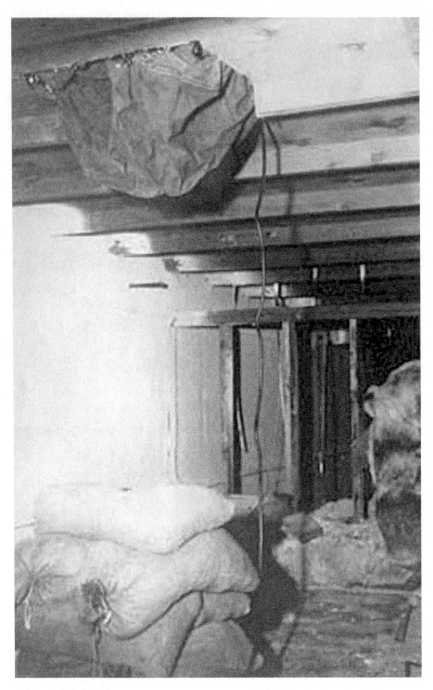

On top of the vault

Hole in the ceiling of the vault

/ 164 / Photographs

Inside the vault

Empty safety deposit boxes

Exhibit 112 - A

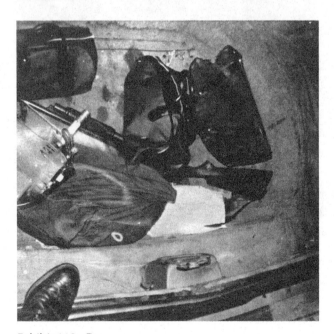

Exhibit 112 - D

Exhibit 112 - E

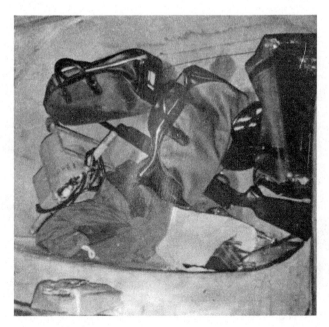

Exhibit 112 - F

Monarch Bay Plaza, Laguna Nigel, circa 1965-67. *(Photo courtesy of Orange County archives)*

Pacific Coast Highway, Laguna Nigel, 1980. *(Photo courtesy of Jay Philippbar, personal collection)*

For more information,
please visit my website,
http://amildinsio.com